Keep this pocket-sized
you are travelling aroun

Whether you are in
enjoy an evocative journ ... Compare
the South Dorset of old with what you can see today—see how the streets have changed, how shops and buildings have been altered or replaced, how seaside resorts and fishing harbours have developed and expanded; look at fine details such as lamp-posts, shop fascias and trade signs. See the many alterations to South Dorset that have taken place during our lives, and which we may have taken for granted.

At the turn of a page you will gain fascinating insights into South Dorset's unique history.

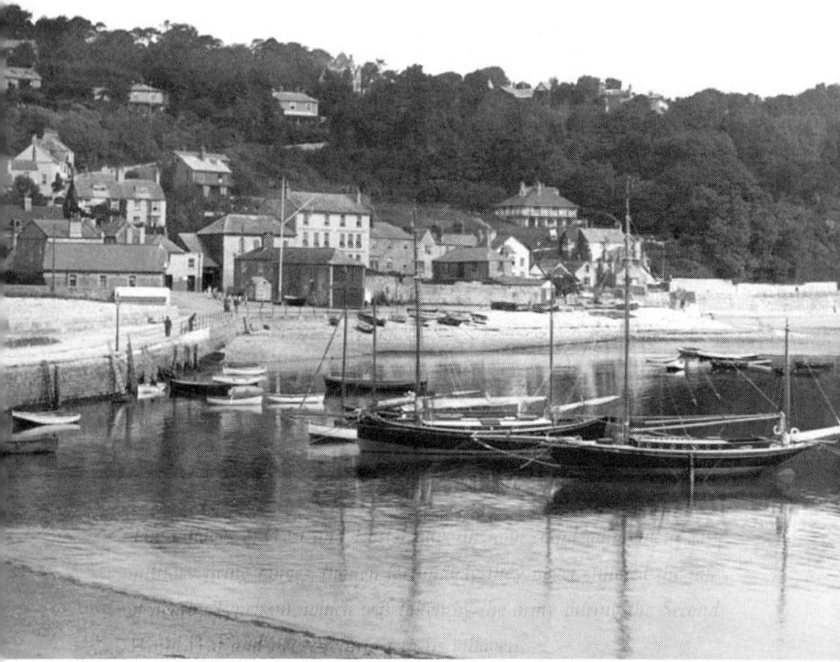

FRANCIS FRITH'S

pocket ALBUM

DORSET COAST

A POCKET ALBUM

Adapted from an original book by
JOHN BAINBRIDGE

THE FRANCIS FRITH COLLECTION

First published in the United Kingdom in 2004 by
Frith Book Company Ltd

ISBN 1-85937-823-4

British Library Cataloguing in Publication Data

Dorset Coast—A Pocket Album
Adapted from an original book by John Bainbridge

Frith Book Company Ltd
Frith's Barn, Teffont,
Salisbury, Wiltshire SP3 5QP
Tel: +44 (0) 1722 716 376
Email: info@francisfrith.co.uk
www.francisfrith.co.uk

Printed and bound in Great Britain by MPG, Bodmin

Front Cover: BOSCOMBE, The Bathing Beach 1925 78783

The colour-tinting is for illustrative purposes only, and is not intended to be historically accurate.

Frontispiece: LYME REGIS, The Harbour 1912 65039

AS WITH ANY HISTORICAL DATABASE THE FRITH ARCHIVE IS CONSTANTLY BEING CORRECTED AND IMPROVED AND THE PUBLISHERS WOULD WELCOME INFORMATION ON OMISSIONS OR INACCURACIES

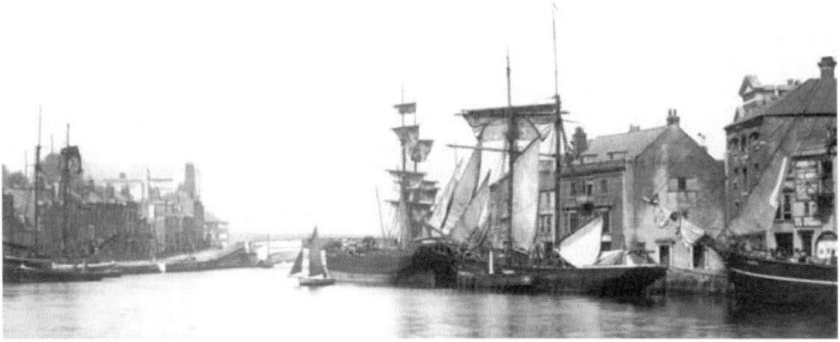

CONTENTS

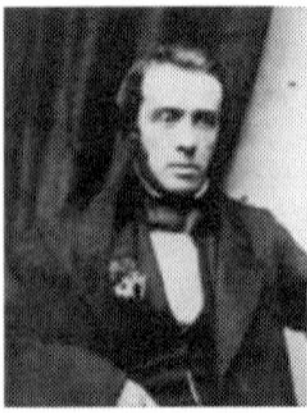

FRANCIS FRITH

VICTORIAN PIONEER

Francis Frith, founder of the world-famous photographic archive, was a complex and multi-talented man. A devout Quaker and a highly successful Victorian businessman, he was philosophic by nature and pioneering in outlook. By 1855 he had already established a wholesale grocery business in Liverpool, and sold it for the astonishing sum of £200,000, which is the equivalent today of over £15,000,000.Now in his thirties, and captivated by the new science of photography, Frith set out on a series of pioneering journeys up the Nile and to the Near East.

INTRIGUE AND EXPLORATION

He was the first photographer to venture beyond the sixth cataract of the Nile. Africa was still the mysterious 'Dark Continent', and Stanley and Livingstone's historic meeting was a decade into the future. The conditions for picture taking confound belief. He laboured for hours in his wicker dark-room in the sweltering heat of the desert, while the volatile chemicals fizzed dangerously in their trays. Back in London he exhibited his photographs and was 'rapturously cheered' by members of the Royal Society. His reputation as a photographer was made overnight.

VENTURE OF A LIFE-TIME

By the 1870s the railways had threaded their way across the country, and Bank Holidays and half-day Saturdays had been made obligatory by Act of Parliament. All of a sudden the working man and his family were able to enjoy days out, take holidays, and see a little more of the world.

With typical business acumen, Francis Frith foresaw that these new tourists would enjoy having souvenirs to commemorate their days out. For the next thirty years he travelled the country by train and by pony and trap, producing fine photographs of seaside resorts and beauty spots that were keenly bought by millions of Victorians. These prints were painstakingly pasted into family albums and pored over during the dark nights of winter, rekindling precious memories of summer excursions. Frith's studio was soon supplying retail shops all over the country, and by 1890 F Frith & Co had become the greatest specialist photographic publishing company in the world, with over 2,000 sales outlets, and pioneered the picture postcard.

FRANCIS FRITH'S LEGACY

Francis Frith had died in 1898 at his villa in Cannes, his great project still growing. The archive he created continued in business for another seventy years. By 1970 it contained over a third of a million pictures showing 7,000 British towns and villages.

Frith's legacy to us today is of immense significance and value, for the magnificent archive of evocative photographs he created provides a unique record of change in the cities, towns and villages throughout Britain over a century and more. Frith and his fellow studio photographers revisited locations many times down the years to update their views, compiling for us an enthralling and colourful pageant of British life and character.

We are fortunate that Frith was dedicated to recording the minutiae of everyday life. For it is this sheer wealth of visual data, the painstaking chronicle of changes in dress, transport, street layouts, buildings, housing, engineering and landscape that captivates us so much today, offering us a powerful link with the past and with the lives of our ancestors.

Computers have now made it possible for Frith's many thousands of images to be accessed almost instantly. The archive offers every one of us an opportunity to examine the places where we and our families have lived and worked down the years. Its images, depicting our shared past, are now bringing pleasure and enlightenment to millions around the world a century and more after his death.

DORSET COAST

AN INTRODUCTION

TO JOURNEY along the coastline of Dorset is to travel back in time, for few landscapes in England show as much evidence of either their geological origins, or the multitude of civilisations that have lived and worked upon the fields and clifftops, as this ancient countryside does. Dorset is a county of rolling downlands, deep wooded valleys, and some of the most picturesque towns and villages to be found in the south of Britain.

This is a territory familiar to millions of people throughout the world who may not ever have visited it, for it is immortalised in the novels and poems of Thomas Hardy, Jane Austen, John Fowles and the Powys Brothers; it has also been pictured by hundreds of artists of all abilities. For this is a land that cries out for interpretation: its lonely coves, hilltop forts and tranquil downs and meadows seem to throw out stories, characters and scenic beauty in a way that inspires the artistic mind. The photographic essays of the Frith family capture this mood in all its subtleties.

The Dorset Coast Path follows the coastline from Lyme Regis to Poole, and a walk along it, with suitable diversions inland, is the best way to experience the county as the Friths would have known it. The waves still beat on the shingle shore, curlews still cry above the marshlands, and the sheep still graze on the downs. This is an ancient land, old when the Romans came. Invaders, journeymen workers, merchants, sailors, rebels and artists have all come and gone; and now locals and tourists alike delight in this old county.

LYME REGIS

1890 / 27342

Lyme Regis, seen here from the heights of Timber Hill, is situated at the westernmost end of Dorset. Walking through the fields and cliffs of Lyme the visitor can never be quite sure whether he or she is in Dorset or neighbouring Devon. Some residents at the far end of town are Devonians, while the rest are 'Dorset Good and True'.

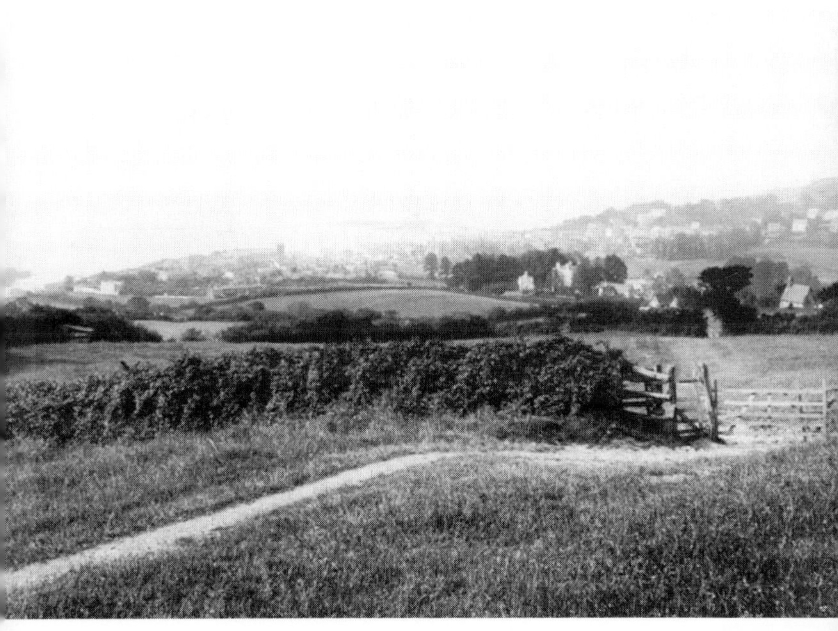

Visitors approaching from Devon descend this steep hill to the sea at Lyme. Broad Street is the town's most fashionable shopping street, though the busy traffic of today prevents dogs lying down in the road!

LYME REGIS

BROAD STREET 1905 / L121001

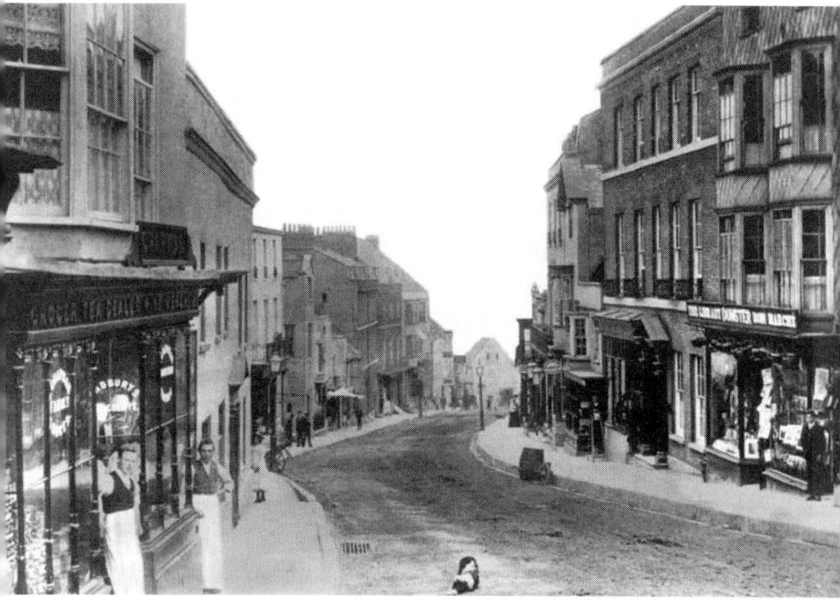

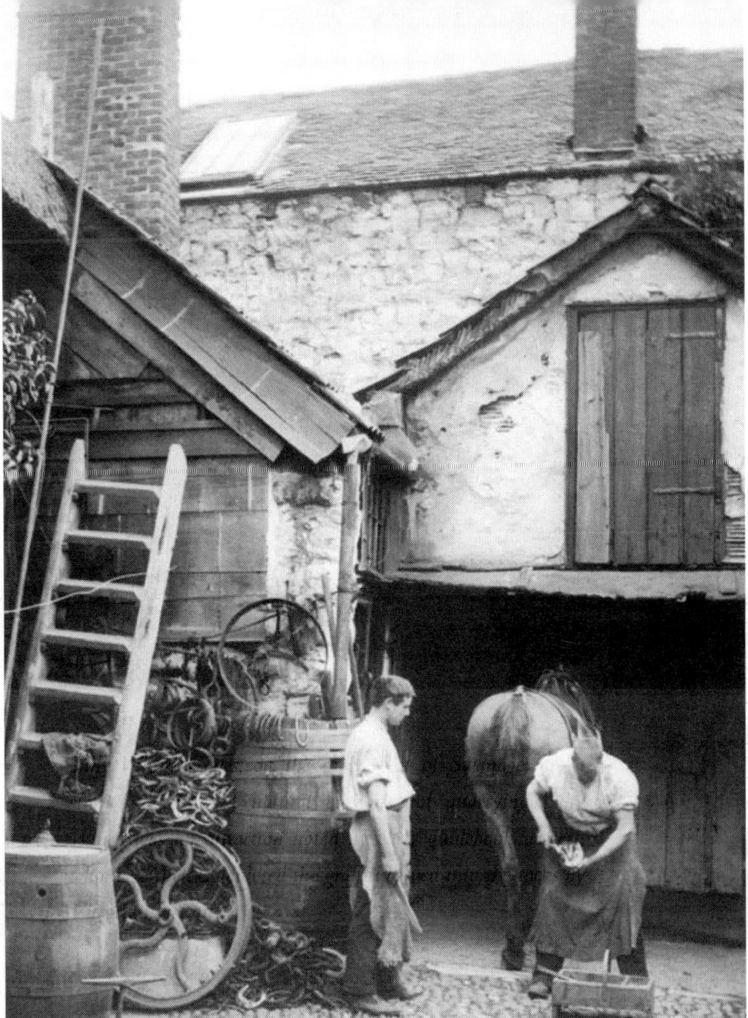

LYME REGIS

SAMUEL GOVIER'S SMITHY 1909 / 61633A

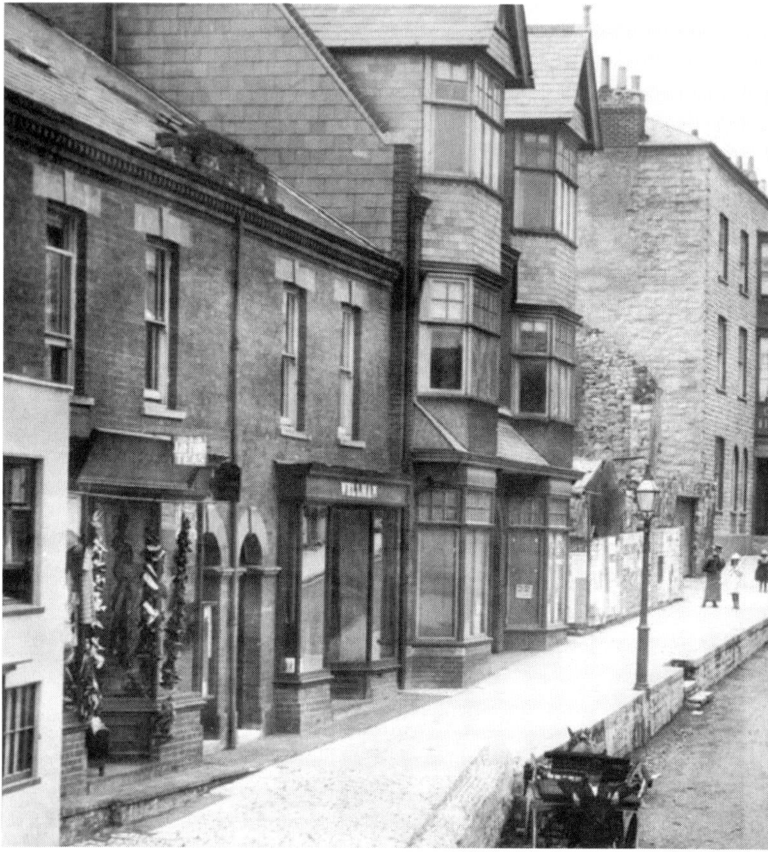

LYME REGIS

BROAD STREET 1900 / 45242

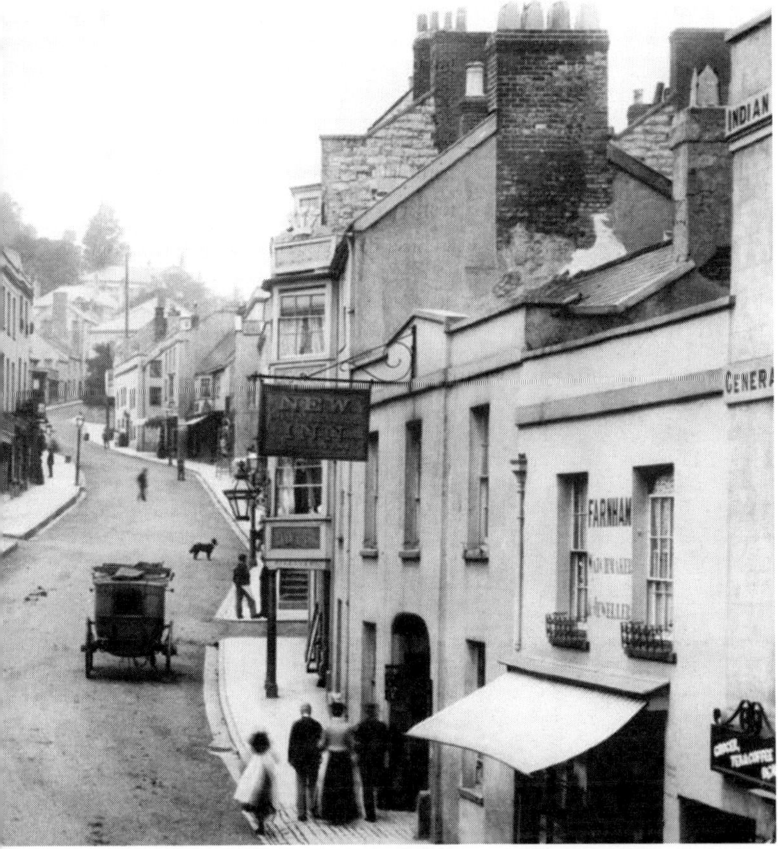

Visitors approaching from Devon descend this steep hill to the sea at Lyme. Looking up Broad Street one can see a great variety of inns and hotels. Famous visitors to Lyme have included Daniel Defoe, Mary Mitford, Jane Austen, Alfred Tennyson and Beatrix Potter. More recently, John Fowles immortalised the town in his famous novel 'The French Lieutenant's Woman'.

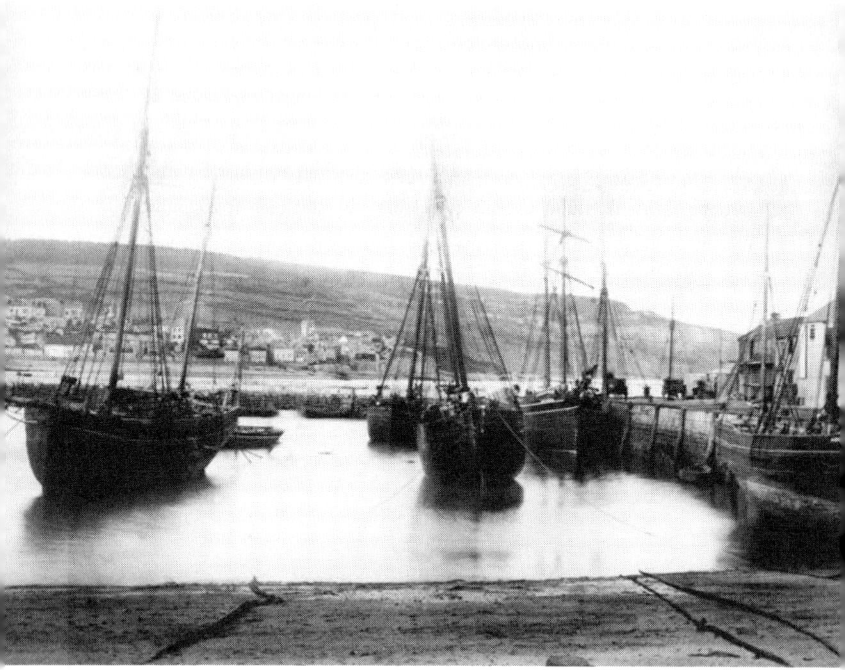

When the nearby harbour of Axmouth fell into disuse after a cliff-fall in the 12th century, the only alternative was to extend the harbour at Lyme Regis. 'There is not any harbour like it in the world', the topographer Roger North exclaimed in 1582, as he described the new docks at Lyme. By the Victorian age, hundreds of ships were trading in and out of Lyme every year.

LYME REGIS

THE HARBOUR 1892 / 31308

At this time the Crown and Anchor Inn, the large building at the foot of the hill, was still open and a focus for community life in Lyme Regis. With its congested, narrow streets, this is by far the oldest part of the town, having been built on land given to Sherborne Abbey by the Wessex king Cynewulf in 774.

LYME REGIS

SHERBORNE LANE 1907 / 58099

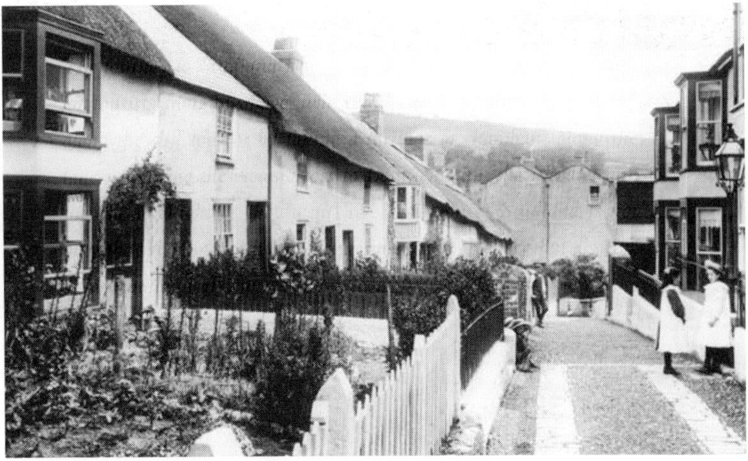

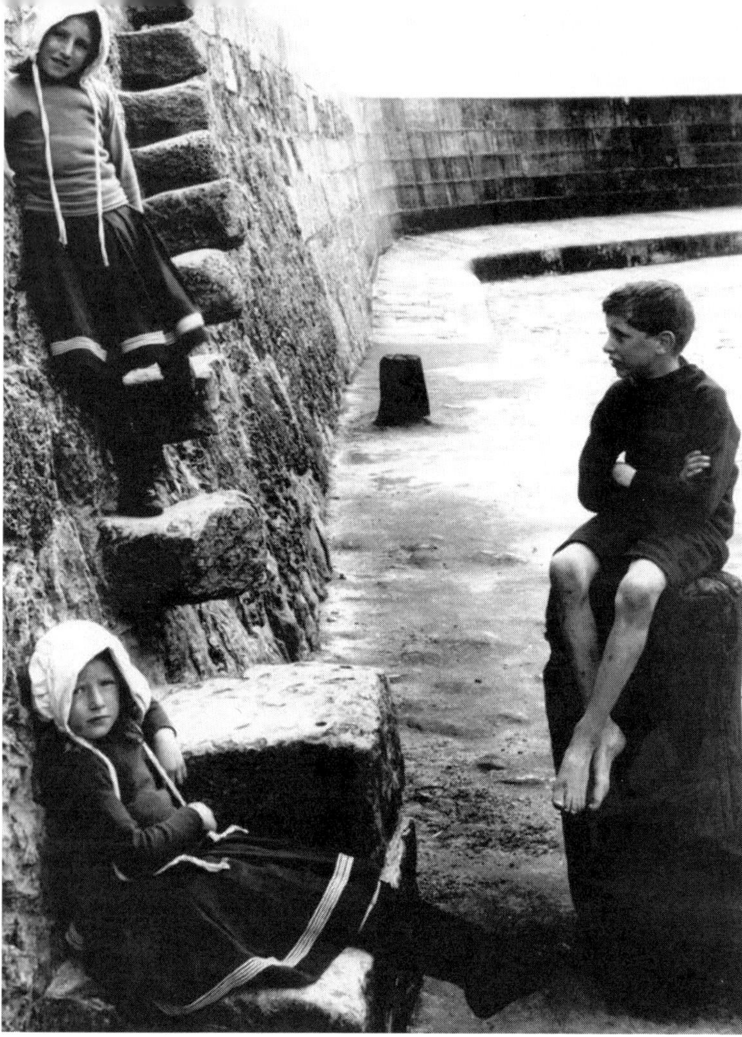

LYME REGIS

THE COBB 1912 / 65040

The old tracks from the neighbouring village of Uplyme are the original routes into the town before the construction of the present road along the coast. Down the tracks packhorses would have brought wool and cloth to the harbour, and rebels would have wearily tramped to join the Duke of Monmouth's army, which gathered in the town in 1685. Jane Austen probably caught her first glimpse of the town from one of these old routes.

LYME REGIS

IN THE LANES 1892 / 31311

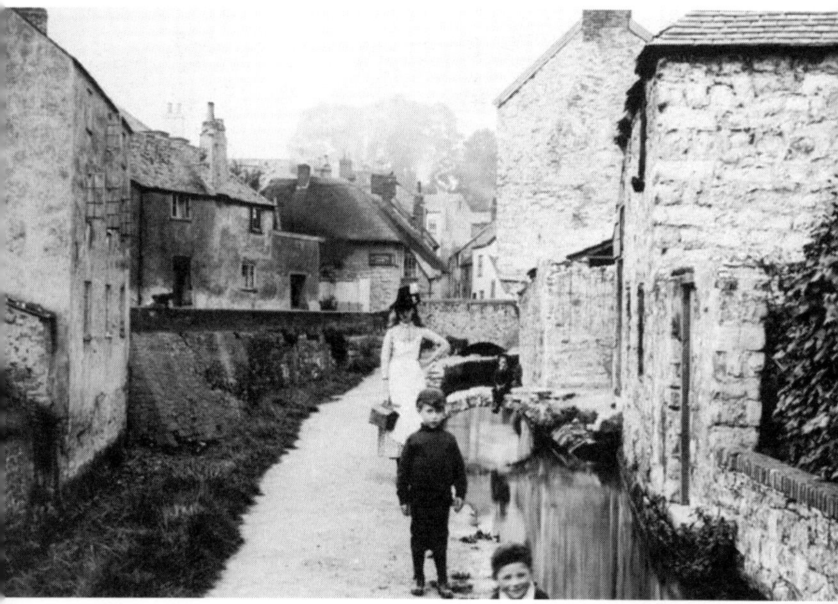

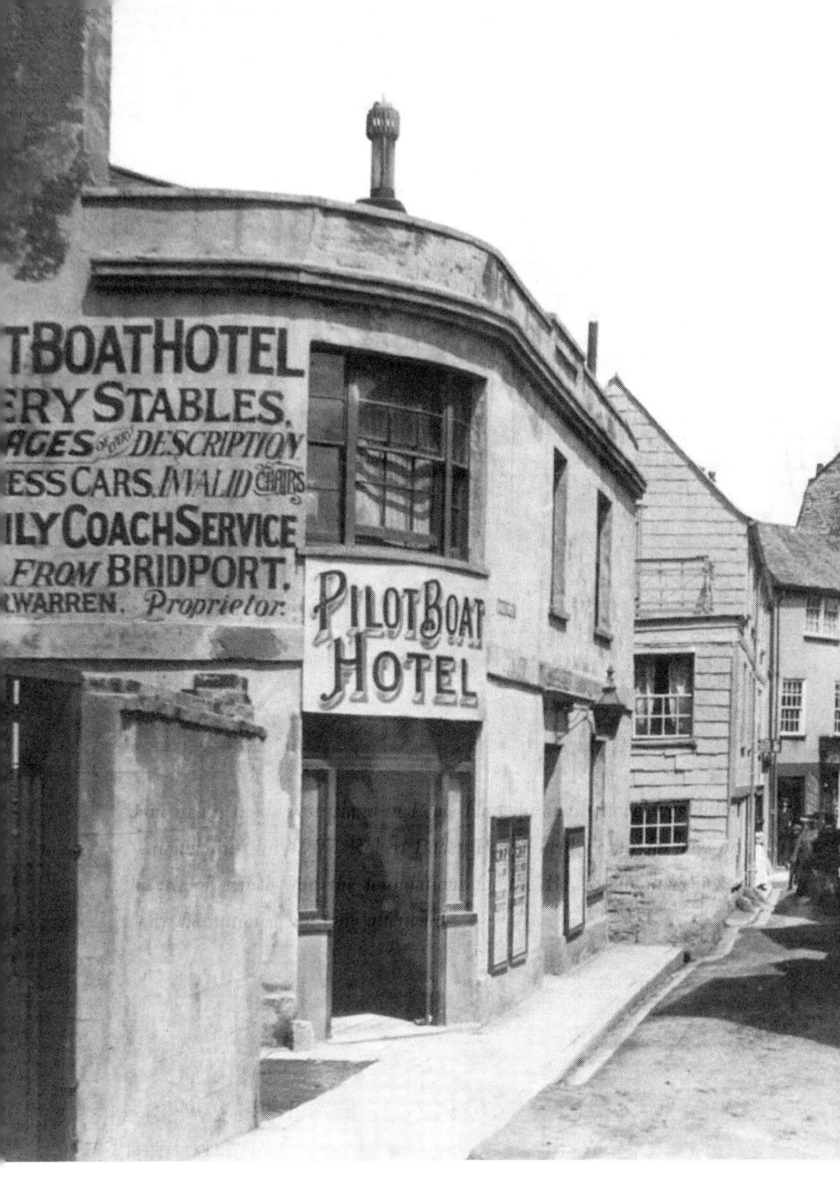
TBOATHOTEL
ERY STABLES.
AGES DESCRIPTION
ESS CARS. INVALID CHAIRS
ILY COACH SERVICE
FROM BRIDPORT.
WARREN. Proprietor.
PILOT BOAT
HOTEL

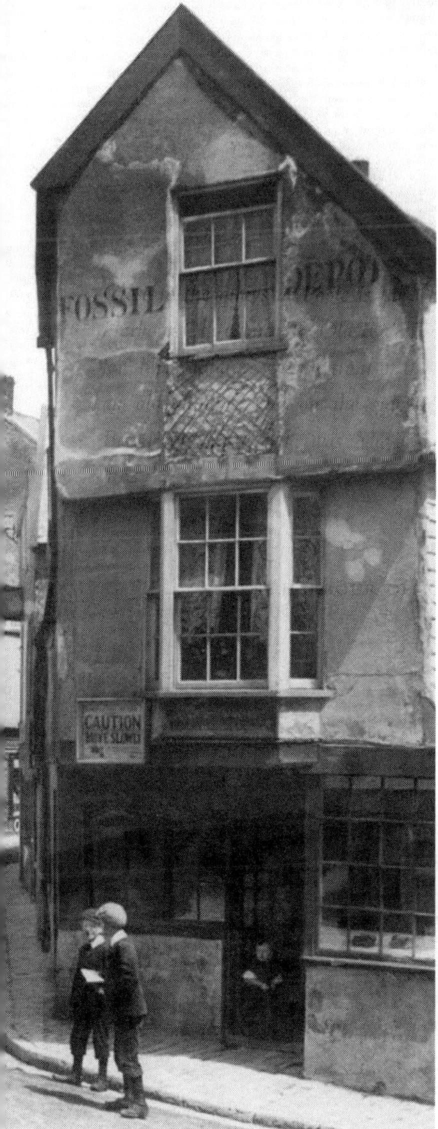

Bridge Street is still one of the narrowest main roads in Dorset. As early as 1909 visitors were coming to Lyme Regis in search of fossils. The Fossil Depot shown here on the right was the first permanent fossil shop in Lyme. It was demolished when Bridge Street was widened in 1913.

LYME REGIS

BRIDGE STREET 1909 / 61625

The Alexandra Hotel was established in 1888 and still welcomes guests today. The building was originally the home of William Pinney MP in the days of ancient boroughs, when Lyme had its own representative at Westminster. The extensive grounds are now part of the public gardens above Marine Parade.

LYME REGIS

THE ALEXANDRA HOTEL 1909 / 61631

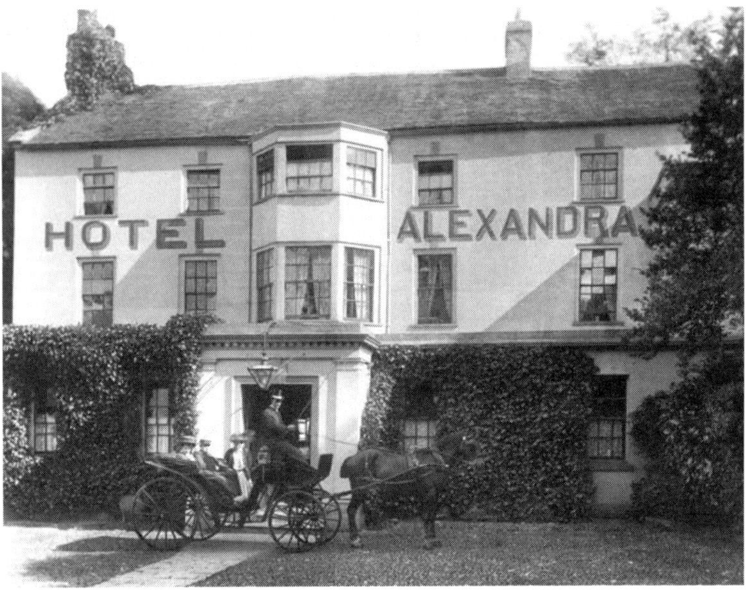

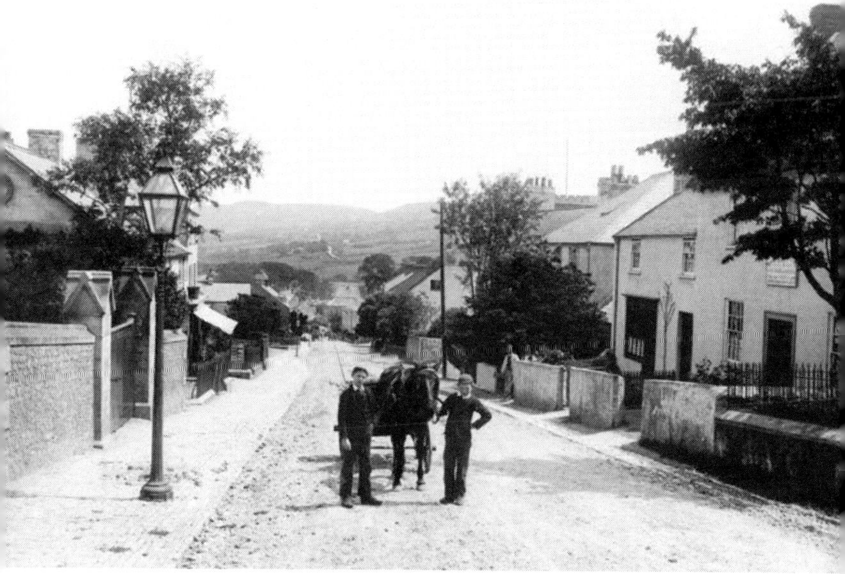

Charmouth village stretches up the long hillside on the western side of the river Char. Few have described the scene as well as Jane Austen in 'Persuasion': 'Charmouth, with its high grounds and extensive sweeps of country, and, still more, its sweet retired bay, backed by dark cliffs, where fragments of low rock among the sands make it the happiest spot for watching the flow of the tide; for sitting in unwearied contemplation'.

CHARMOUTH

THE VILLAGE 1890 / 27380

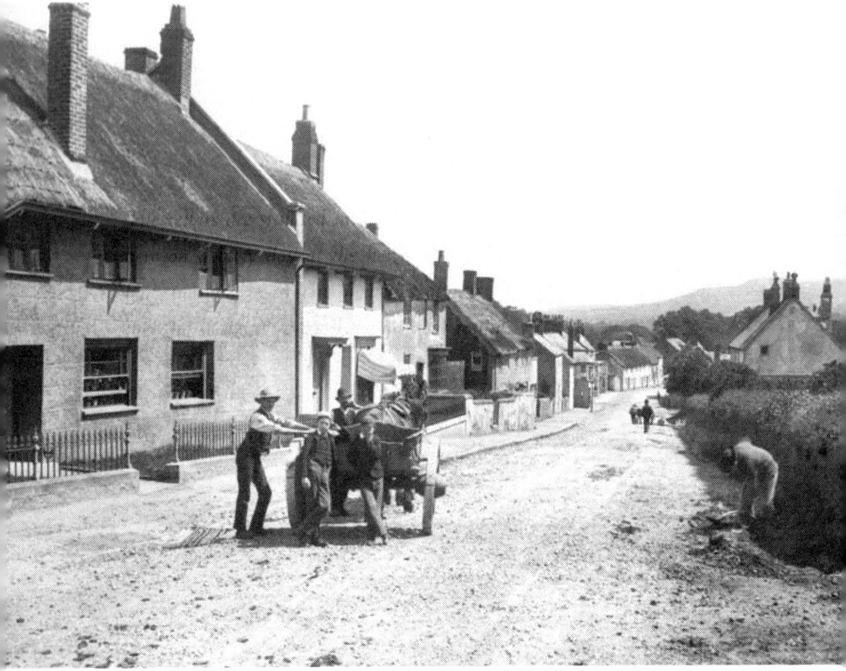

Charmouth was a notable settlement even in Saxon times when two Saxon kings, Egbert and Ethelwulf, fought the Danes nearby. A later king, Charles II, hid here briefly during his escape from the Battle of Worcester. The heart of the village is the steep main street, lined with some splendid bow-windowed cottages.

CHARMOUTH

STREET VIEW 1898 / 27382

Once on the high road between Axminster and Bridport, Charmouth has now been bypassed, but even so the traffic up the steep hill out of the village will never be as quiet as on the peaceful day pictured here.

CHARMOUTH

THE VILLAGE 1900 / 46060

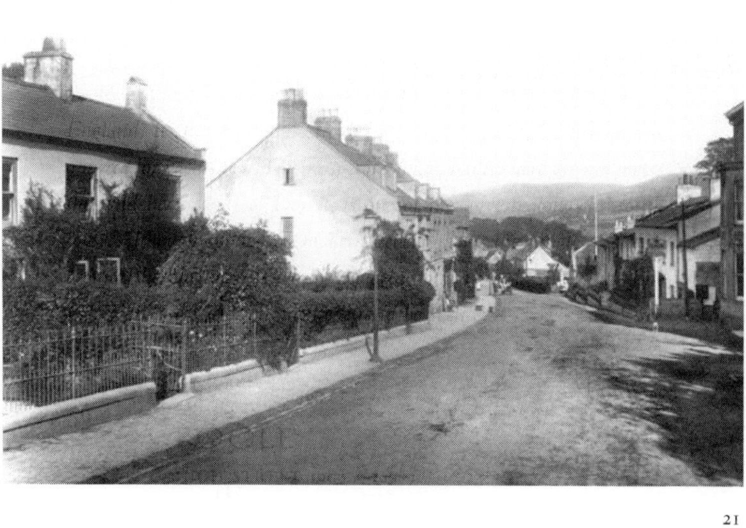

The beach at Charmouth is a mecca for geologists and fossil hunters, and explanatory walks take place from the heritage centre by the mouth of the Char. It was near Charmouth that Mary Anning discovered the remains of an ichthyosaurus in 1811, helping to launch the new science of palaeontology and changing the course of scientific thought.

CHARMOUTH

THE RIVER CHAR c1960 / C66069

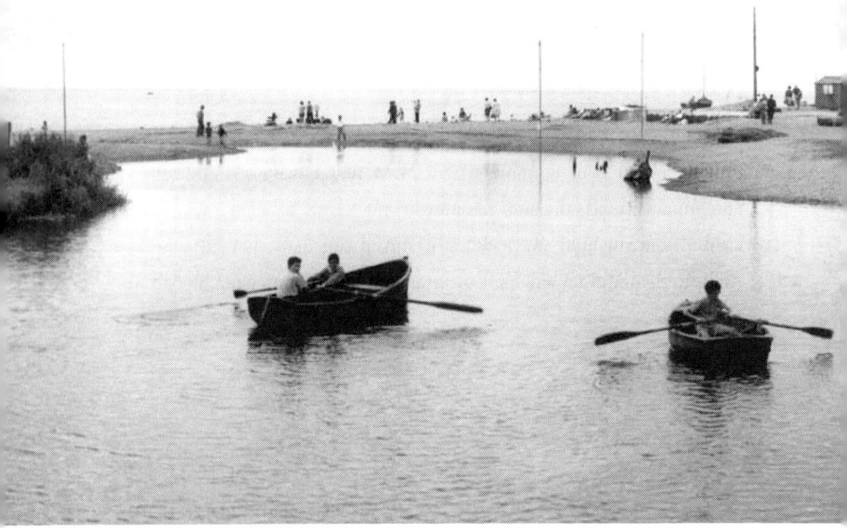

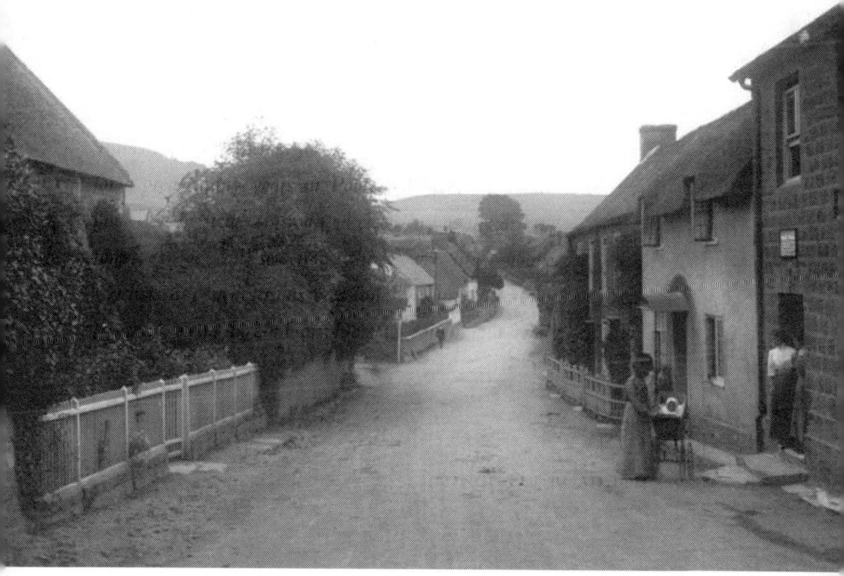

Chideock, usually pronounced without the 'e', stands rooted in history along the line of an old stagecoach route. It was for many years the haunt of Dorset smugglers, who landed their cargoes on the nearby beach of Seatown.

CHIDEOCK

THE VILLAGE 1912 / 65079

CHIDEOCK

THE VILLAGE 1912 / 65080

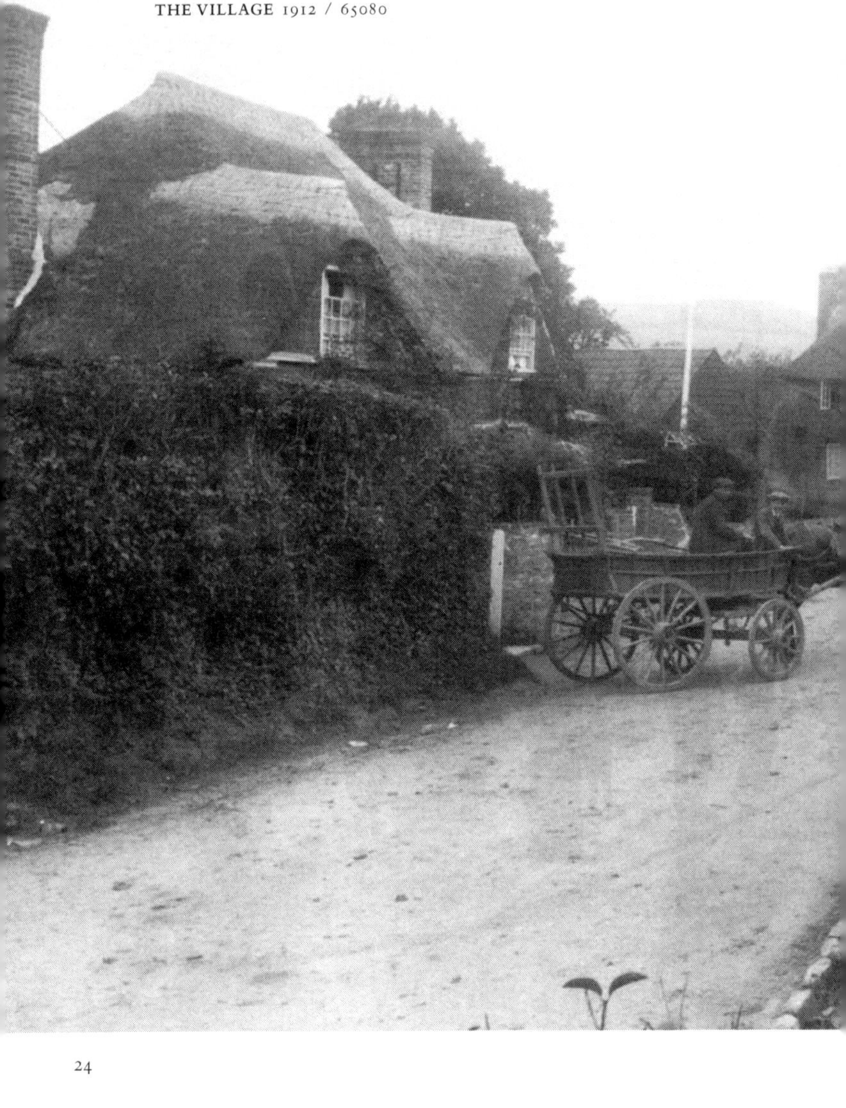

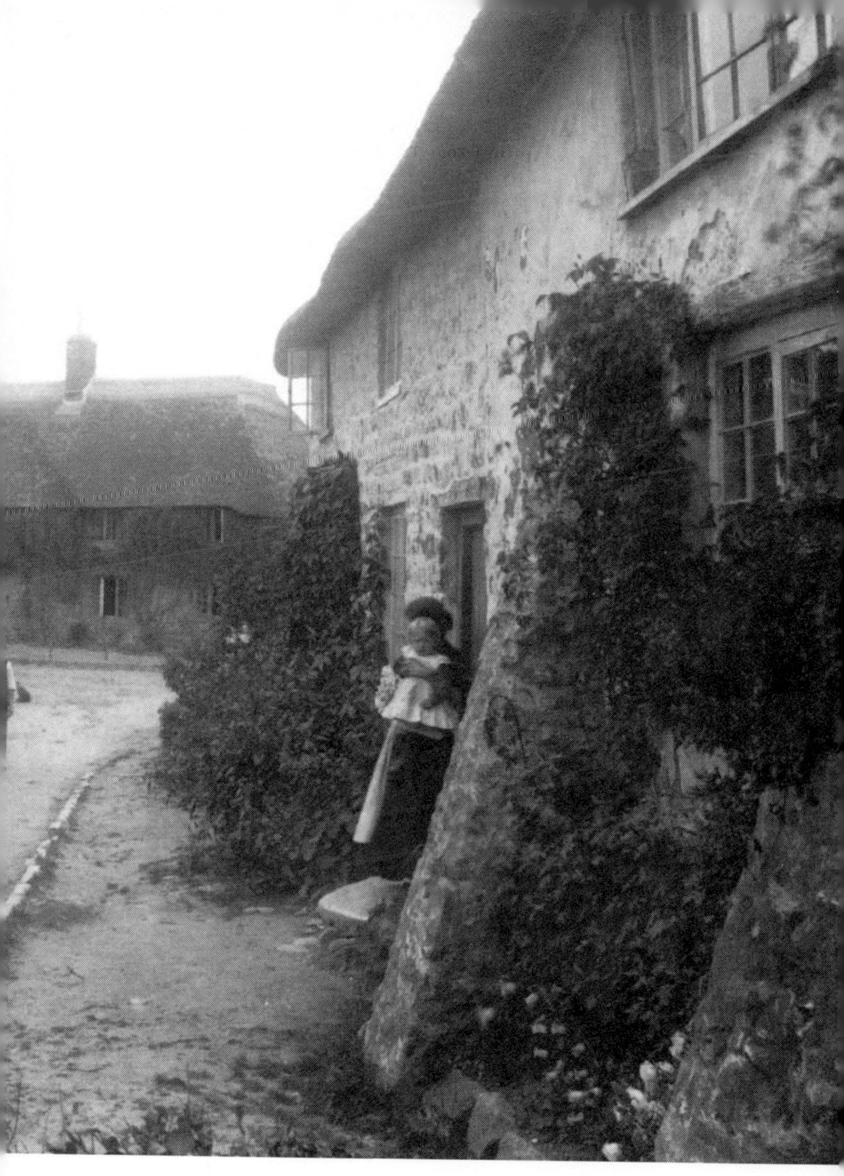

A pastoral scene which might have come from a novel by Thomas Hardy. Harvesters work the fields within the shadow of Netherbury Church in the last peaceful years before the Great War.

NETHERBURY

HAYMAKING BY ST MARY'S CHURCH 1912 / 65068

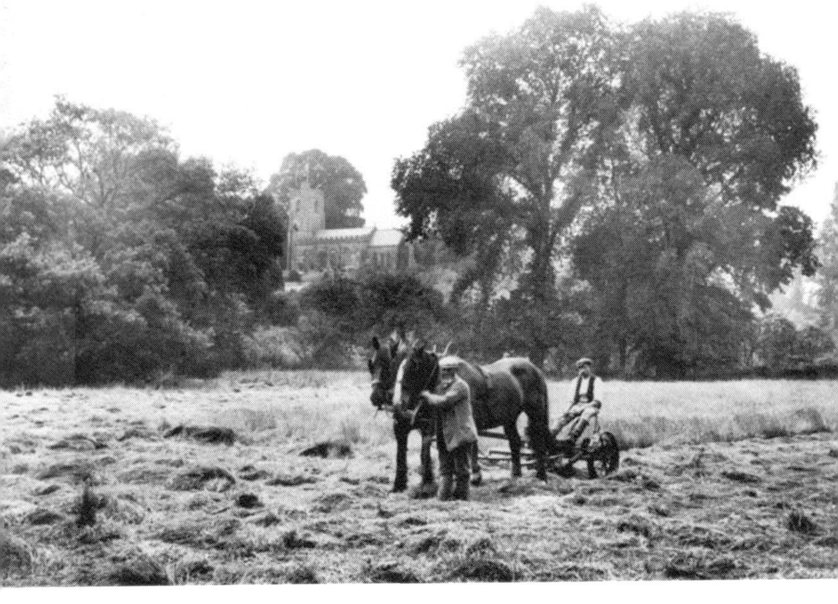

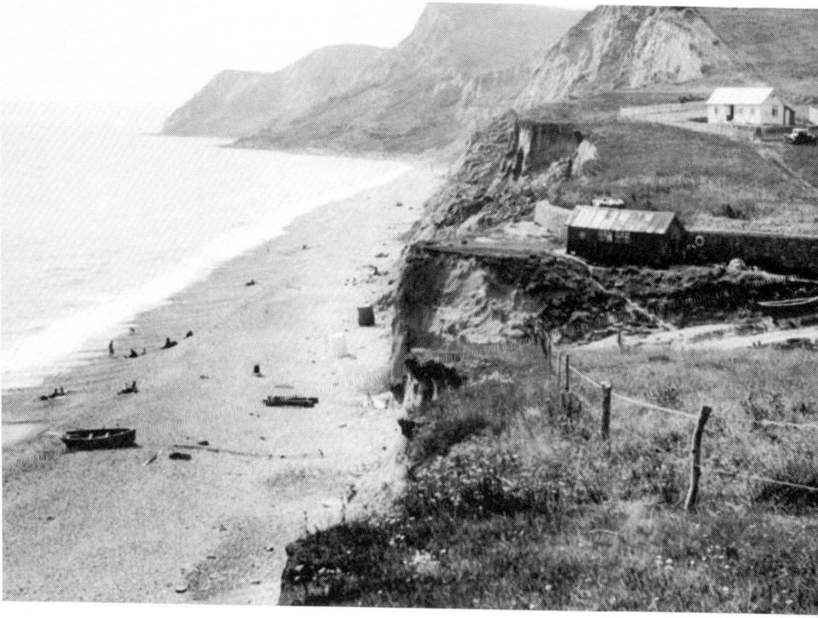

Eype in the days before it was invaded by caravans and the steady influx of tourists who now descend to the beach at Eype Mouth. In days gone by, this wild stretch of coastline would have been known to few except fishermen, shepherds and smugglers.

EYPE

THE BEACH 1930 / 83371

West Bay is the small port of the neighbouring town of Bridport. The River Brit, which gives the larger town its name, is held back by a series of sluices and released at low tide. The swell between the piers as the great waves of Lyme Bay wash into the harbour entrance is an awe-some sight.

WEST BAY

THE QUAY 1897 / 40081

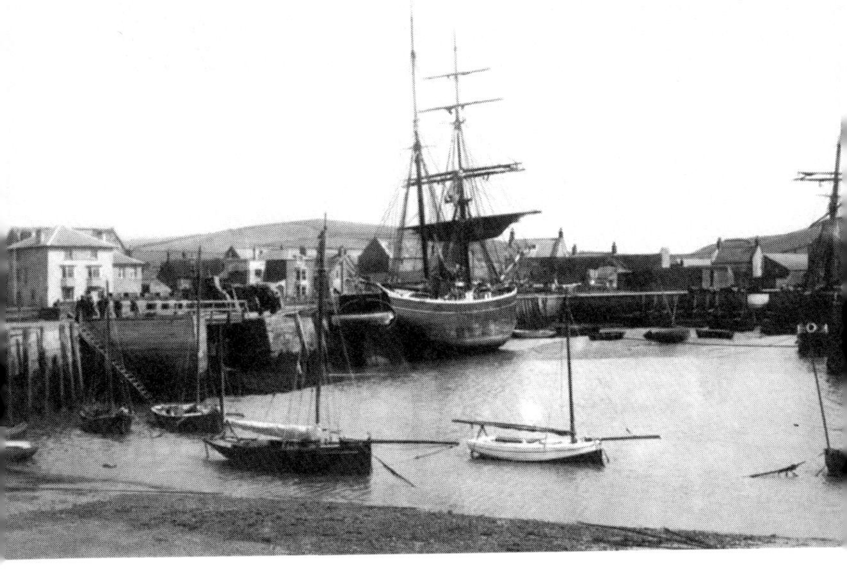

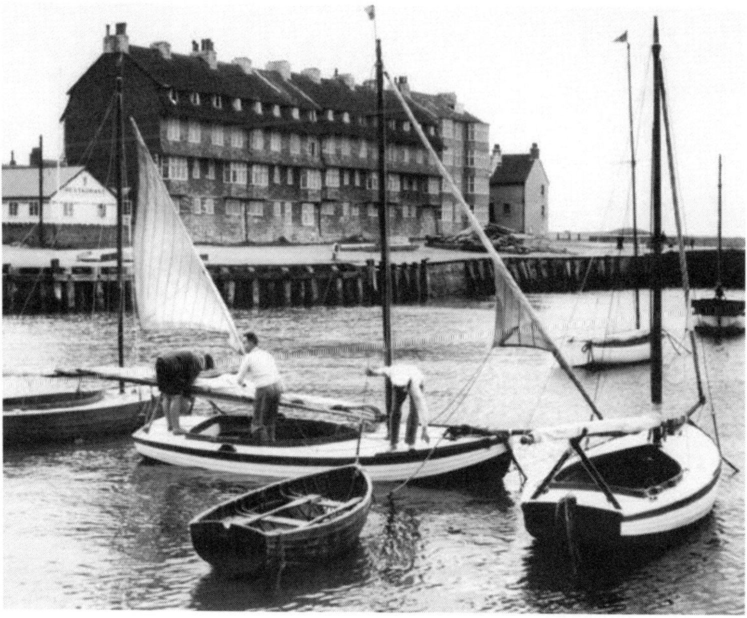

West Bay only acquired its name in the 1880s when the railway was brought down to its picturesque harbour. The larger sailing vessels of late Victorian days have gone, but fishing boats still leave the harbour to bring home their catch, when the swell of the channel allows them to pass through the narrow harbour entrance.

WEST BAY

THE HARBOUR 1930 / 83355

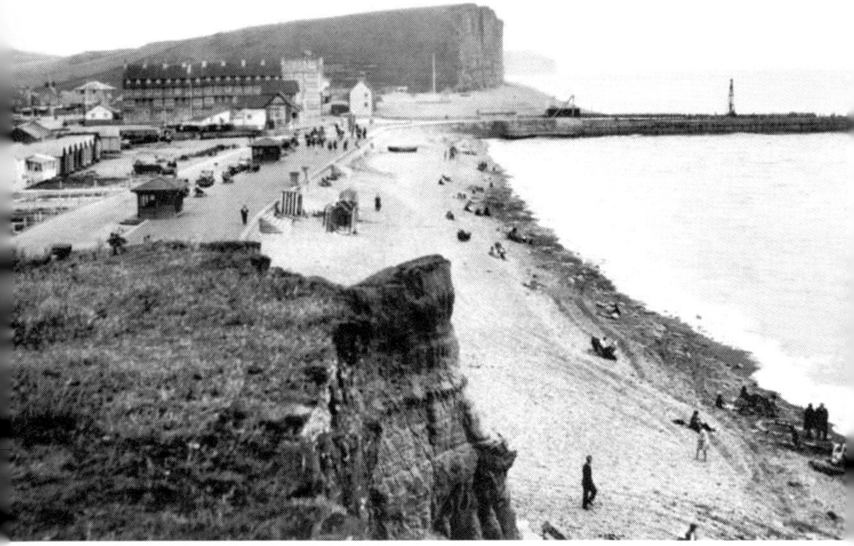

West Bay has now become the setting for a popular television series, 'Harbour Lights', which has brought many more tourists to the village. Attempts by the Victorians to turn West Bay into a leading holiday resort never quite worked, though a great many holiday flats have been built in recent years. However, it is a mecca for day-trippers.

WEST BAY

GENERAL VIEW 1930 / 83349

As long ago as the reign of Edward the Confessor, Bridport was a town of considerable importance, boasting over a hundred dwellings, a priory of monks and its own mint. As its name implies, it was once the port on the River Brit or Bredy, though the original harbour silted up long ago, forcing the construction of the new anchorage at West Bay.

BRIDPORT

FROM ALLINGTON HILL 1897 / 40068

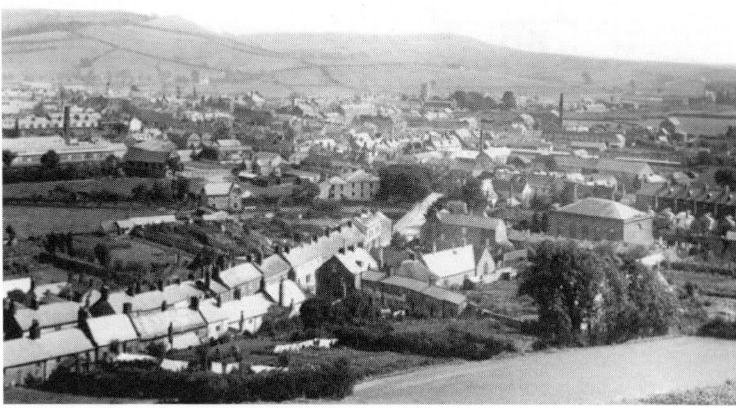

From early times, Bridport was famous for the growing of hemp and the manufacture of rope. In the small streets and alleyways off South Street, the old rope-walks can still be seen. Much of the cordage for Royal Navy vessels was produced in and around Bridport.

BRIDPORT

SOUTH STREET 1897 / 40070

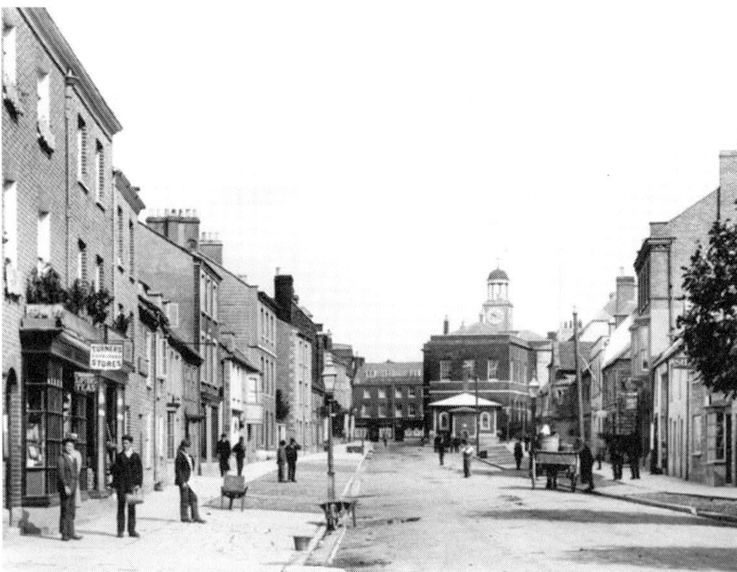

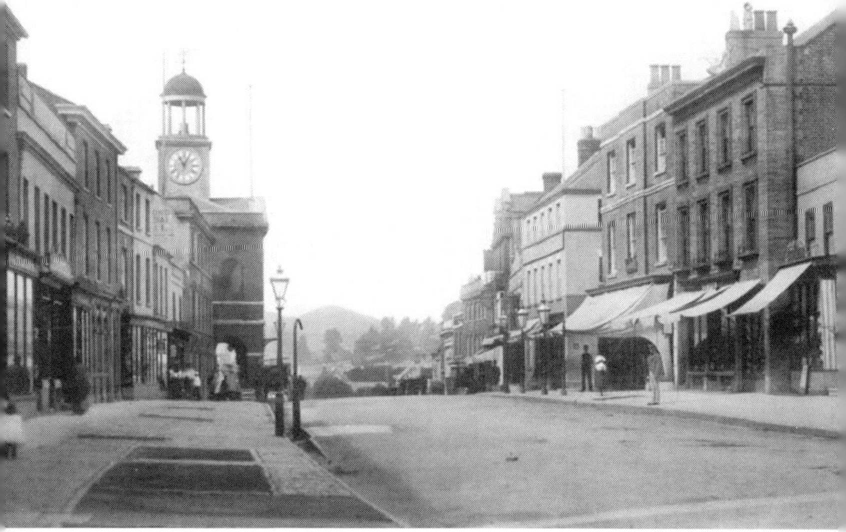

East Street and West treet form part of the old coaching route between Exeter and Dorchester. The wide road shows the importance of this route to the town. The wide pavements are said to have been constructed to facilitate rope and net making outside the inhabitants' houses.

BRIDPORT

EAST STREET 1897 / 40074

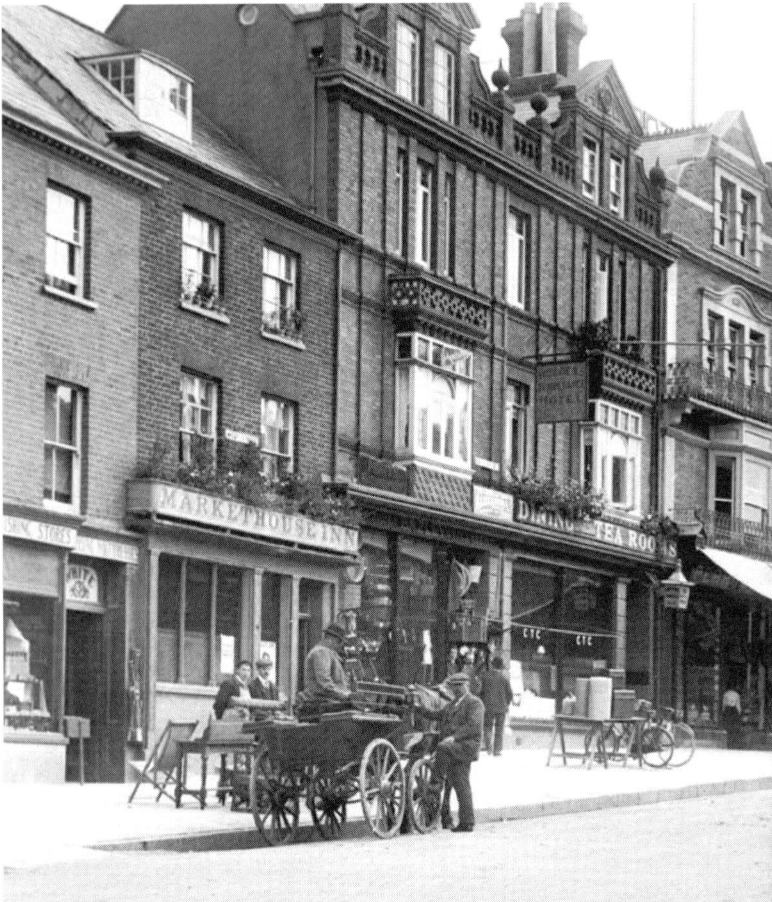

BRIDPORT

EAST STREET 1904 / 52756

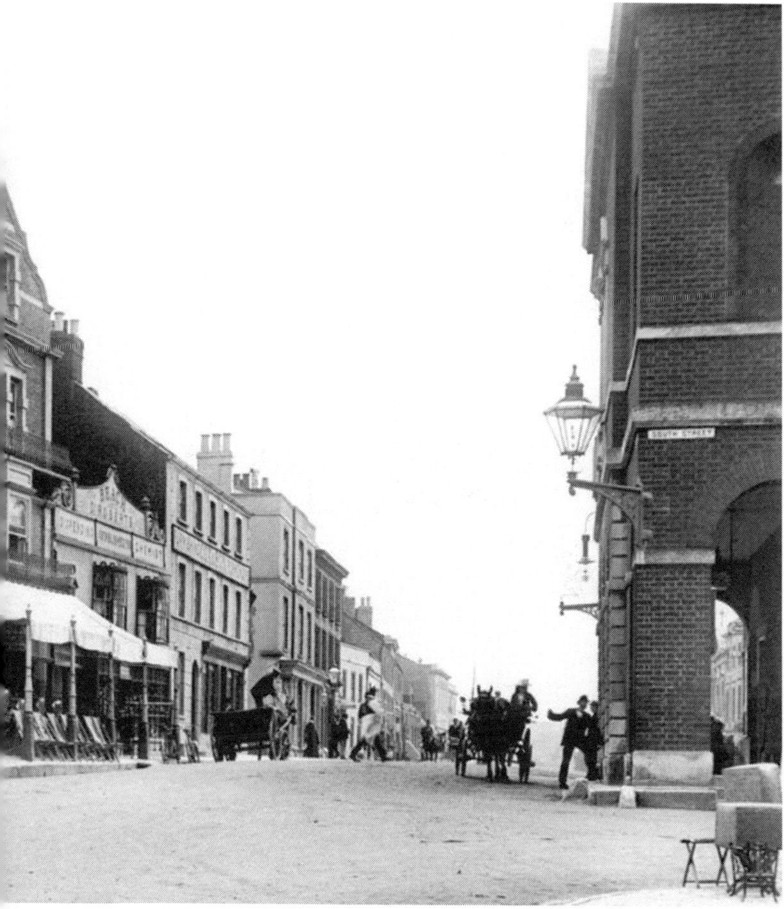

Here we see the junction of East Street and South Street, with the Georgian town hall jutting out onto the highway on the right. Market stalls still line the main street on market days, attracting customers from all over West Dorset.

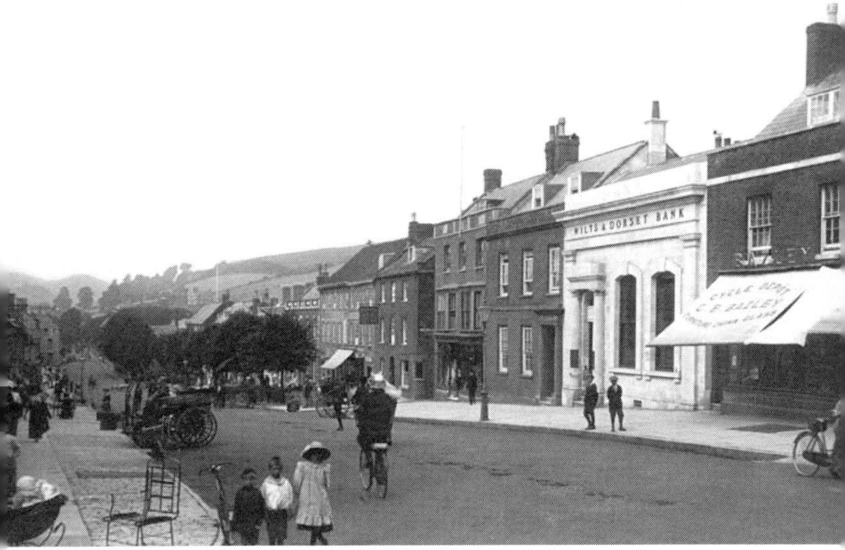

Ropes were made in the alleyways around West Street. The old expression 'to be stabbed by a Bridport dagger' meant to be hanged by a rope made in the town.

BRIDPORT

WEST STREET 1913 / 65643

Once a village in its own right, standing on the slopes above the River Bredy, Bothenhampton has now become a suburb of Bridport. It is best known for the beauty of the architecture of its two churches: the ancient building has been sympathetically restored, and the newer place of worship has four impressive stone arches which rise high above the congregation.

BOTHENHAMPTON

THE VILLAGE 1904 / 52767

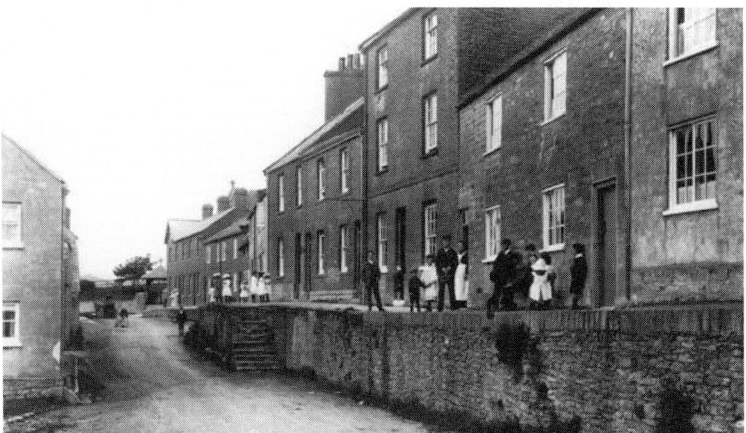

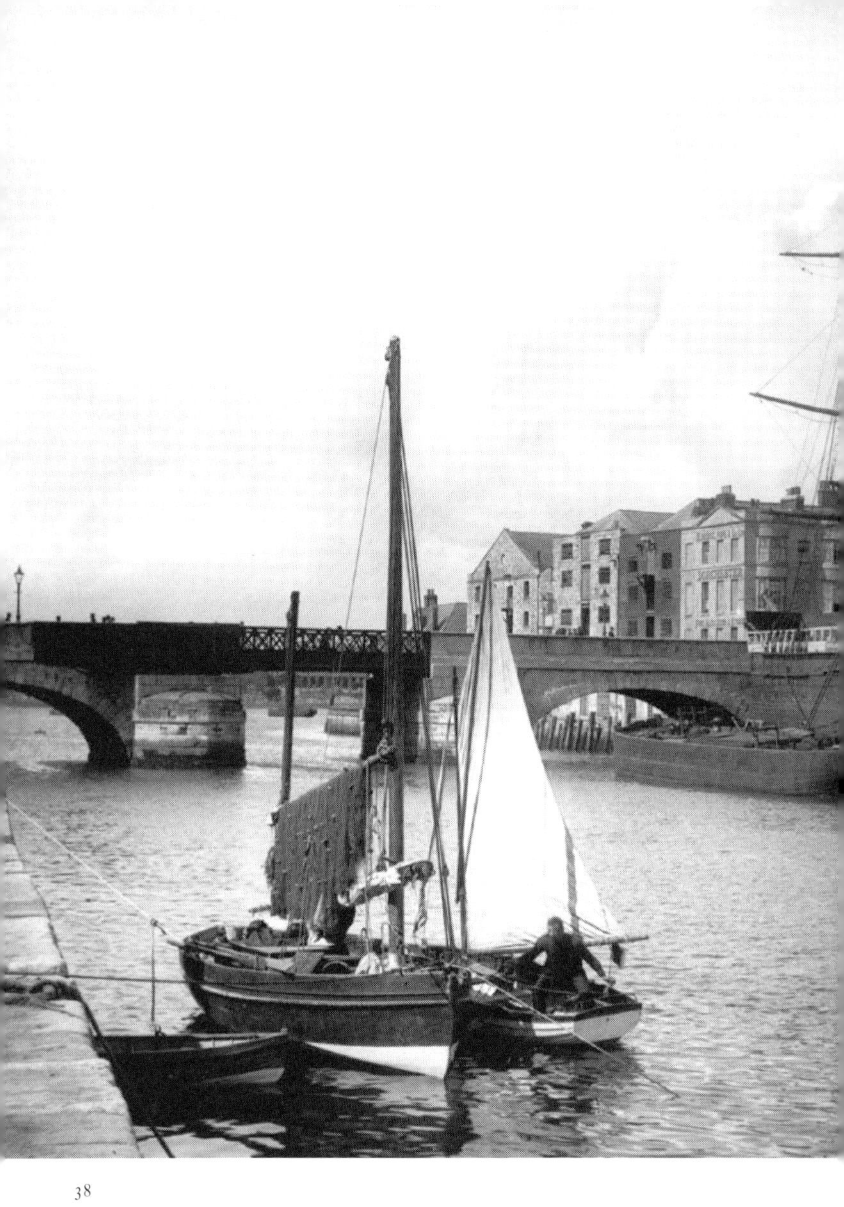

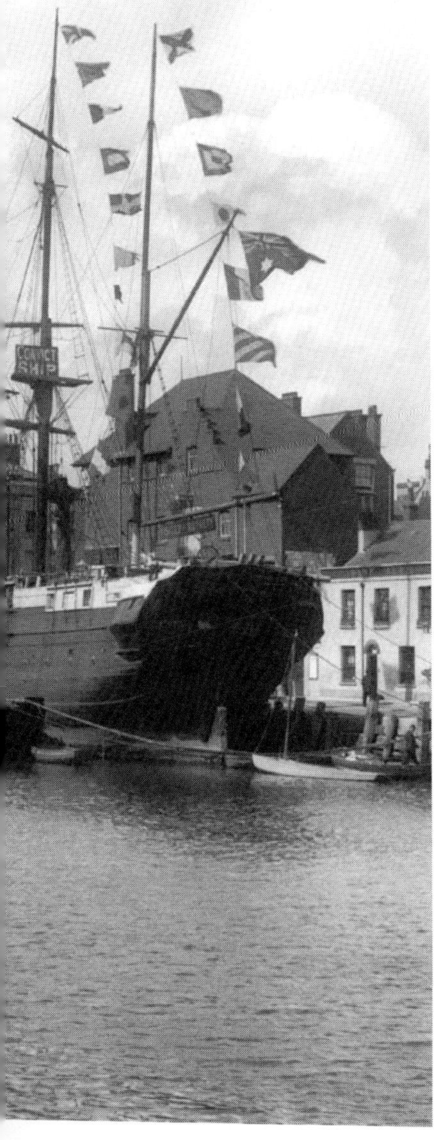

The trade with the Channel Islands and France began soon after the Norman Conquest. It is likely that the inhabitants of inland villages such as Wyke Regis and Melcombe Regis moved nearer the sea to take advantage of these new markets for goods, establishing the present town and harbour at Weymouth. Here, a fine sailing vessel is moored near Weymouth Bridge. The heyday of sail was almost over; steam vessels were replacing the ocean-going ships, but some sailing vessels continued to trade from Weymouth well into the 1920s.

WEYMOUTH

THE HARBOUR 1904 / 52861

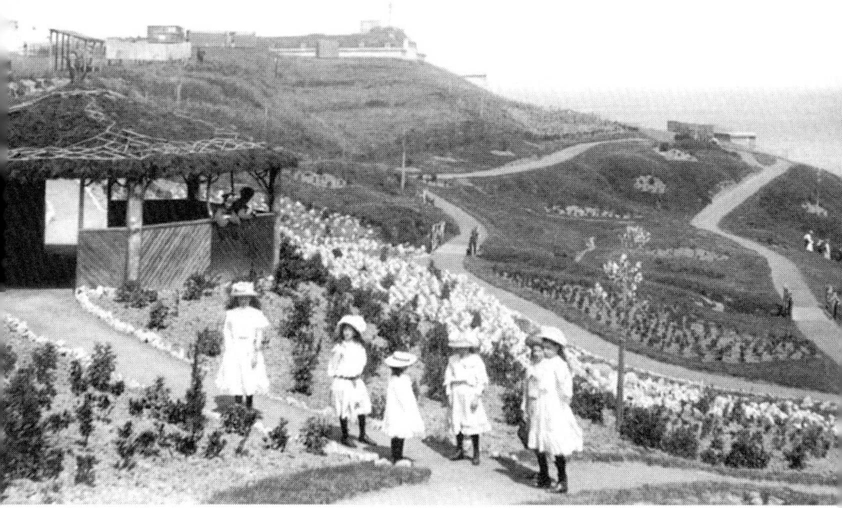

Weymouth's Nothe Gardens are beautifully situated on a headland overlooking the Isle of Portland and are the site of Nothe Fort, built to guard the huge naval harbour between the mainland and the Isle. At the time this view was taken Nothe Fort was equipped with quick-firing guns and could accommodate a battalion of soldiers.

WEYMOUTH

THE NOTHE GARDENS 1909 / 61591

After Weymouth harbour was dredged and improved in 1888, larger ships joined the trade routes between the town and foreign ports. Here we see a paddle steamer moored at the harbour wall. The first steam-paddle driven vessels, the 'Ivanhoe' and 'Warspite', arrived in Weymouth as early as 1827. The ship pictured here is probably one of their successors, built by the famous Lairds yard at Birkenhead in the 1890s.

WEYMOUTH

THE HARBOUR 1898 / 41112

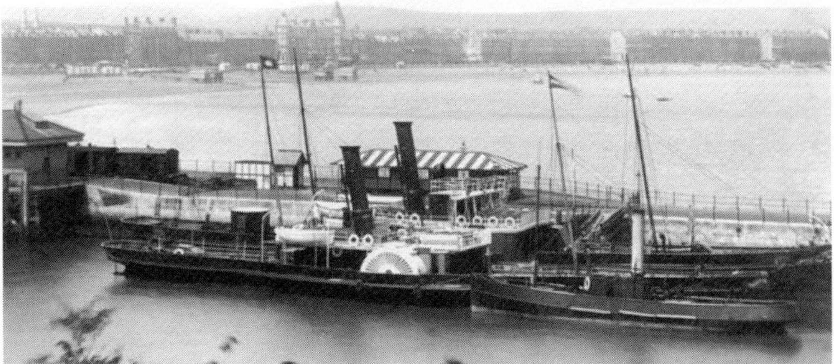

Weymouth became popular as a seaside resort thanks to the patronage of King George III, who came to bathe here for the good of his health. As the king plunged into the waves a brass band, discreetly hidden in a bathing machine, played 'God Save the King'! King George is commemorated by a statue in the town and a carved chalk figure on the hills nearby.

WEYMOUTH

THE PARADE 1898 / 41119

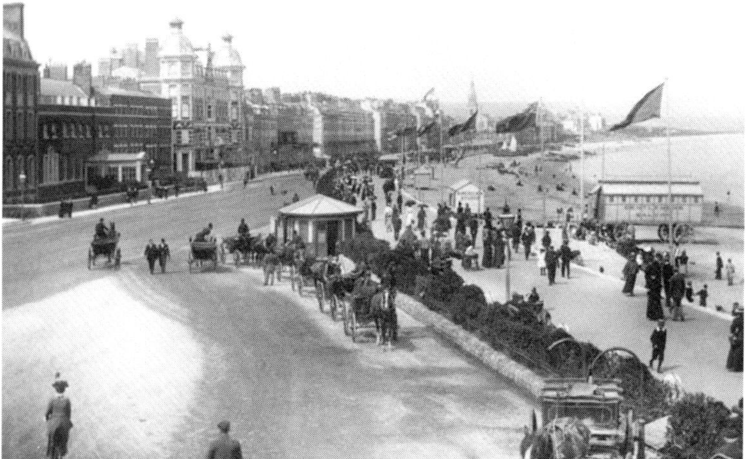

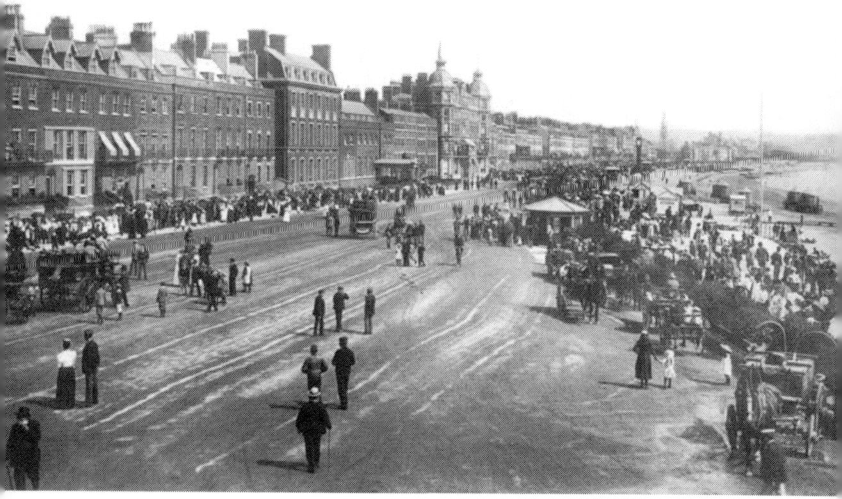

Weymouth, unlike many south coast resorts, faces east; it is therefore possible to sit on hot sunny days without the glare of the afternoon sun in the face. This accounted for the popularity of the long beach and the Esplanade.

WEYMOUTH

THE ESPLANADE 1899 / 43852

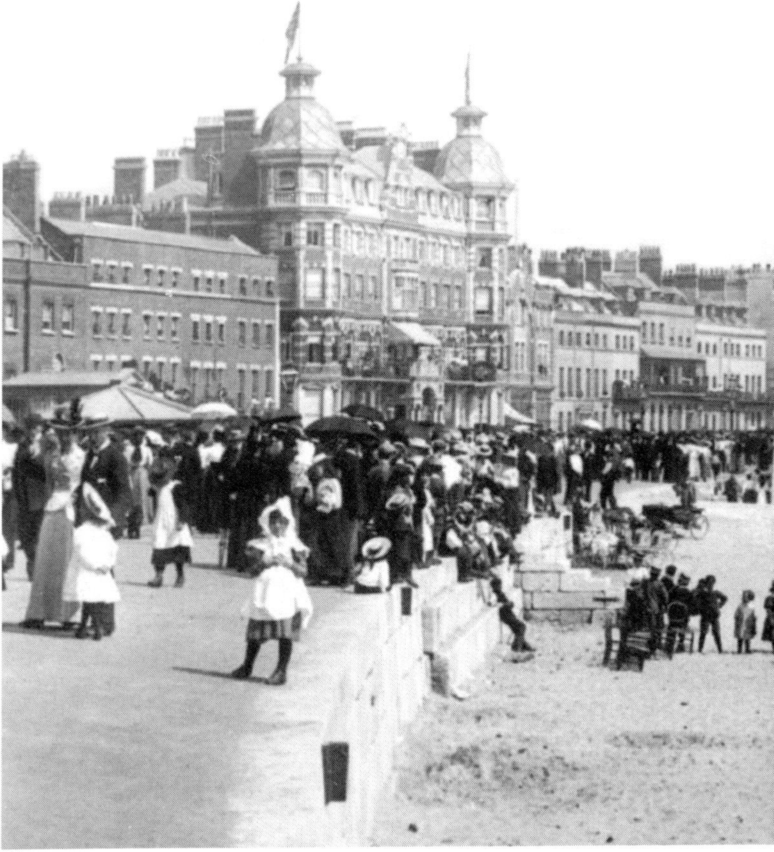

WEYMOUTH

BEACH SHOW 1899 / 43853X

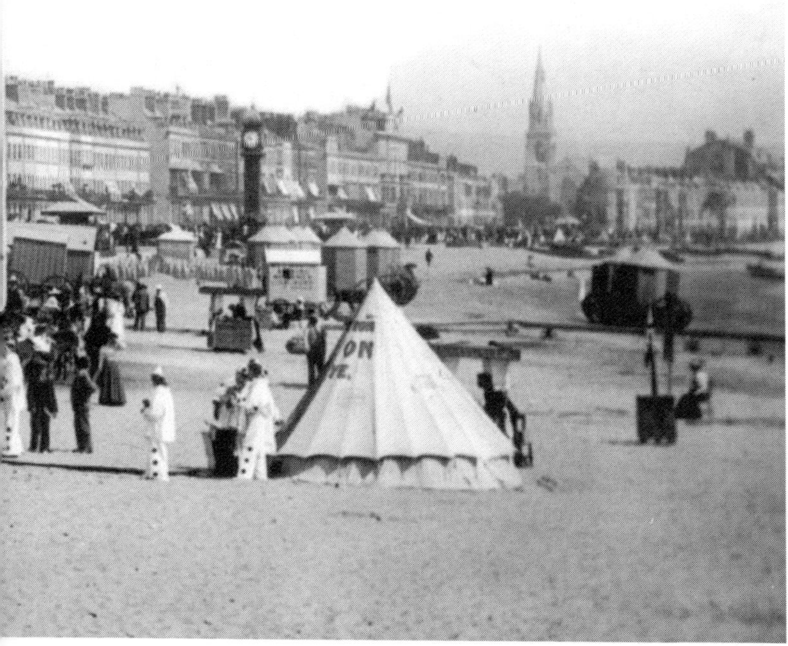

An old guidebook stressed the health benefits of a holiday in Weymouth: 'Weymouth is much more open than the majority of seaside resorts, and is almost surrounded by salt water. This results in an air largely impregnated with ozone and, with the ever-changing tide, ensures a constantly renewed atmosphere.'

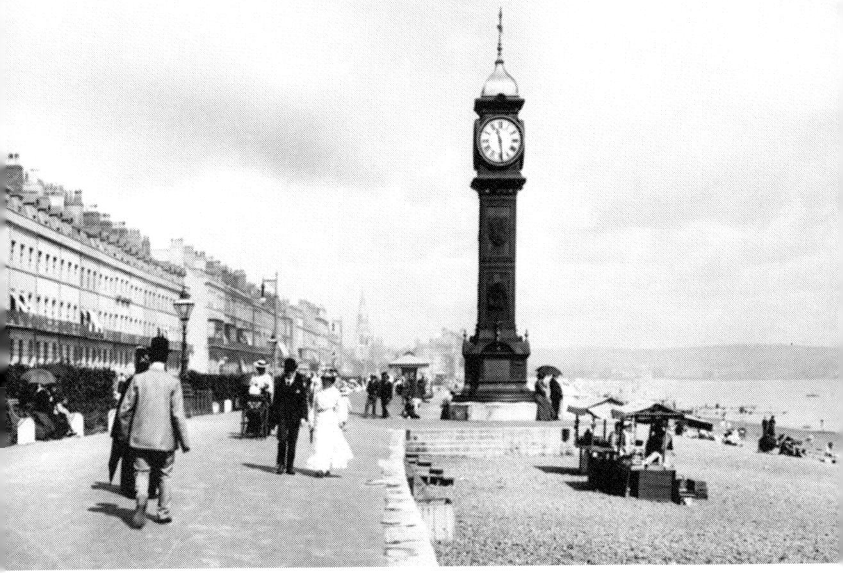

The Parade was built in Georgian times as the fashionable residential quarter of the town. Near here, members of the royal family would stay during and after the reign of George III. In the far distance is the spire of St. John's church, a very prominent landmark from out at sea.

WEYMOUTH

THE PARADE 1904 / 52857

At the entrance to Weymouth Pier stands the Pavilion Theatre, pictured here the year after it opened. The Pavilion quickly eclipsed the other small theatres around the town, offering a variety of plays all the year round. It was constructed with a seating capacity of 1100.

WEYMOUTH

THE PAVILION 1909 / 61594

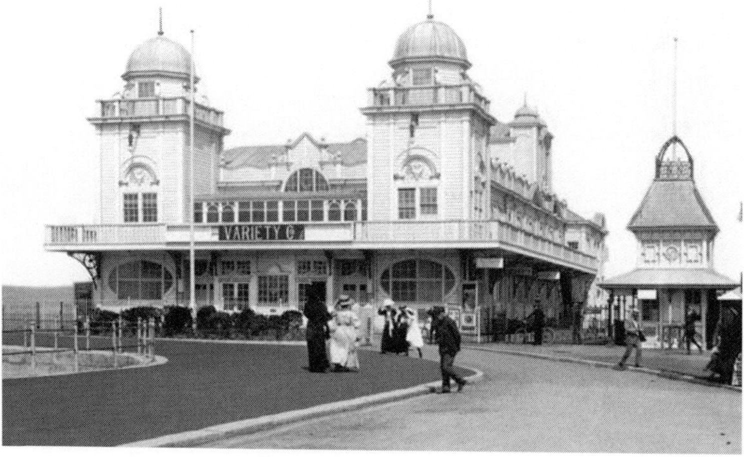

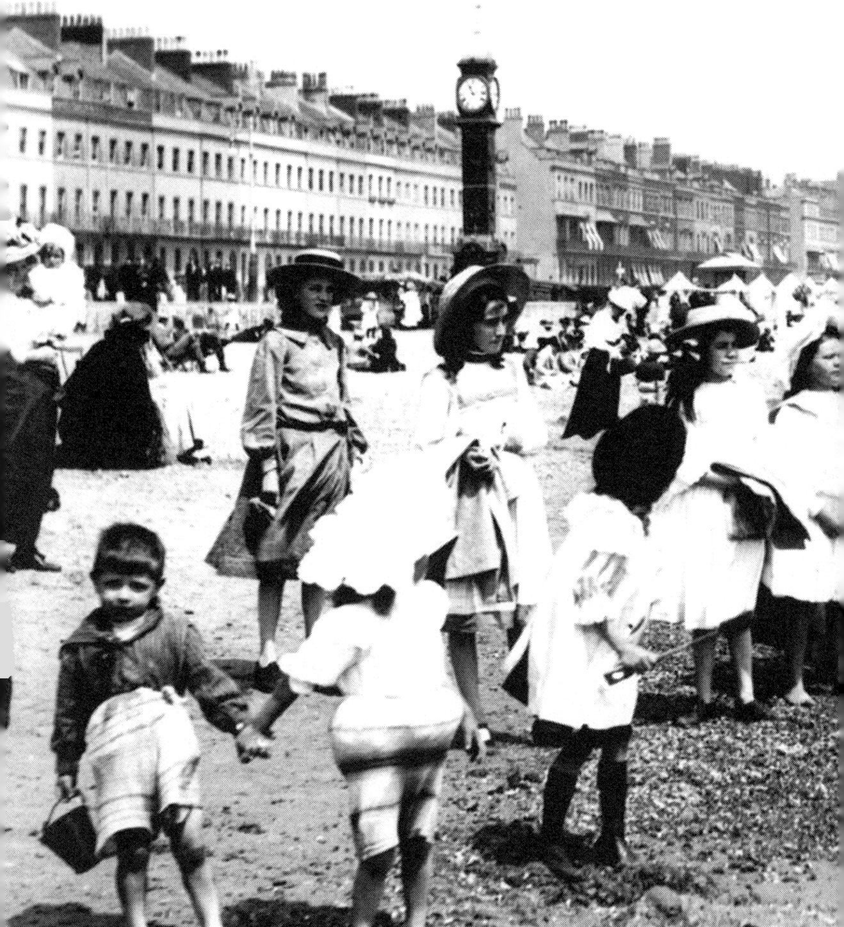

WEYMOUTH

THE SANDS 1909 / 61597

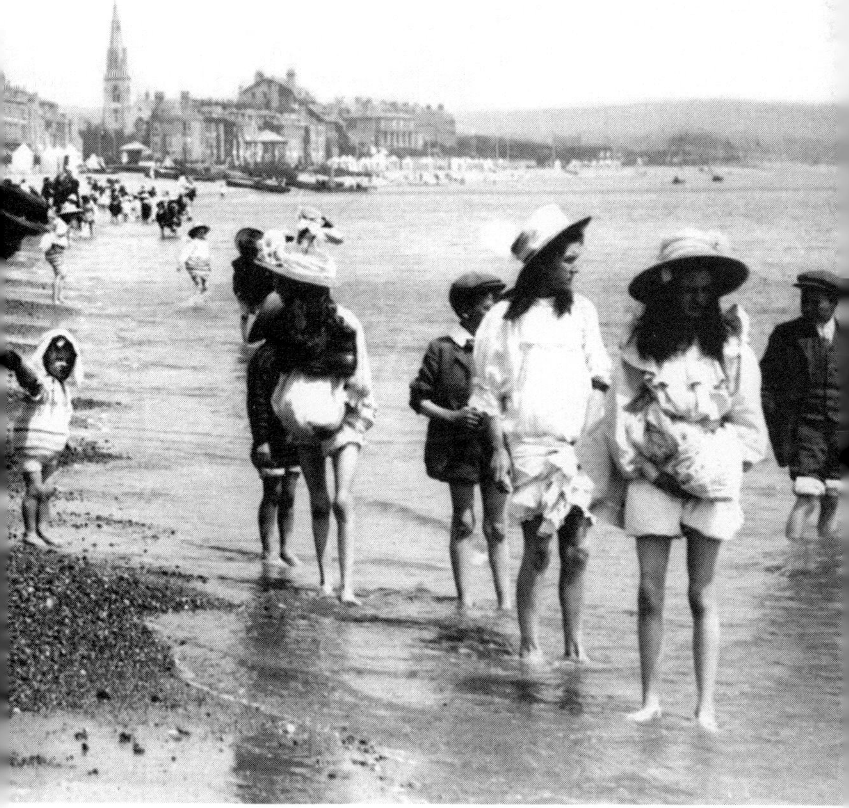

The Esplanade winds around to the Pier and Pavilion Theatre, a favourite stroll for the Edwardian visitor. The pier at this time was 1,050 feet long, and a favoured location for watching the steamers come in and out. The Edwardian visitor would have paid two pence (old currency) to walk to the end of the pier.

WEYMOUTH

THE PIER AND PAVILION 1909 / 61589

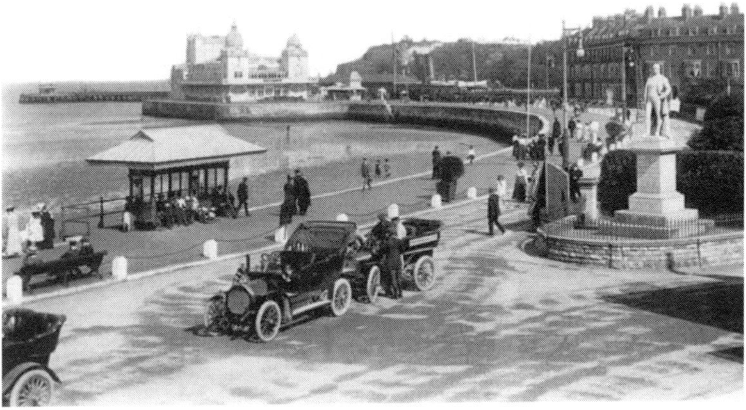

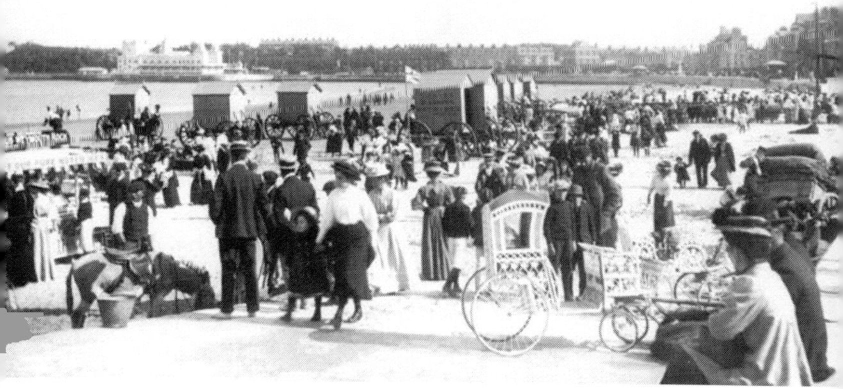

It was the early use of bathing machines that made Weymouth such a popular resort for sea bathing. The larger machines ran down into the water on rails and consisted of a number of cubicles. Affluent visitors would hire a single machine for themselves. Weymouth is constantly likened to the Bay of Naples for the beauty of its setting and the fine curves of its coastline.

WEYMOUTH

THE SANDS 1909 / 61596

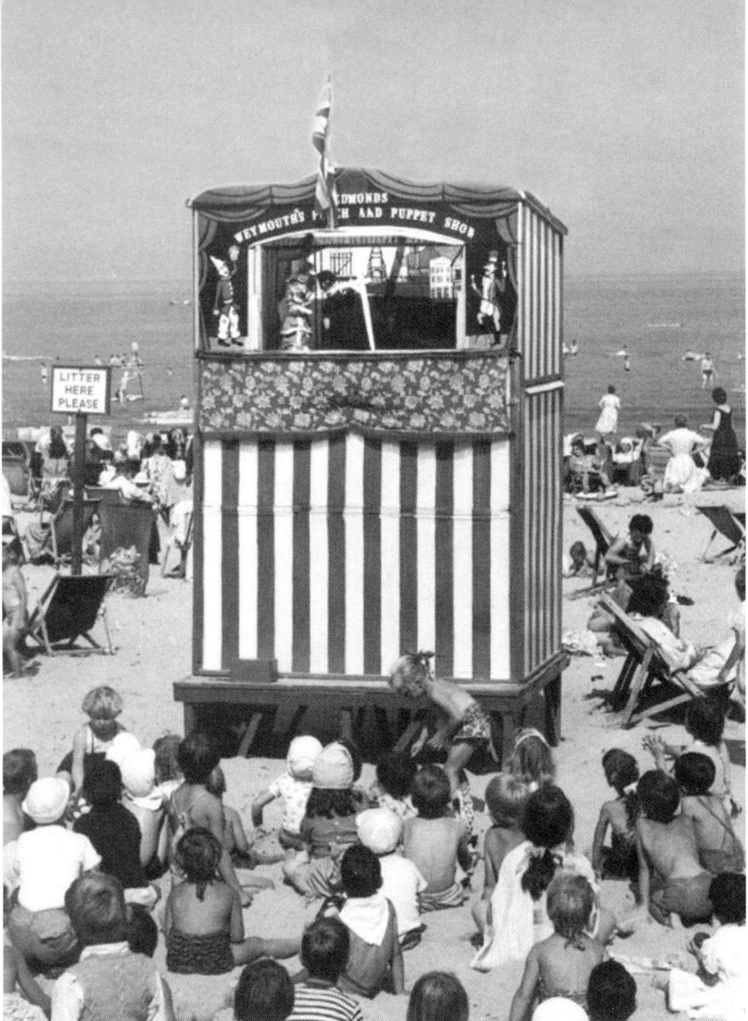

WEYMOUTH

THE PUNCH AND JUDY SHOW c1955 / W76196

The Isle of Portland is more properly a peninsula, which the novelist Thomas Hardy described as 'The Gibraltar of Wessex'. Situated at the end of the long sweep of Chesil Beach, Portland gives shelter to the westerly approaches of Weymouth Bay and is visible for a great many miles up and down the English Channel.

PORTLAND

CHESIL BANK c1875 / 8064

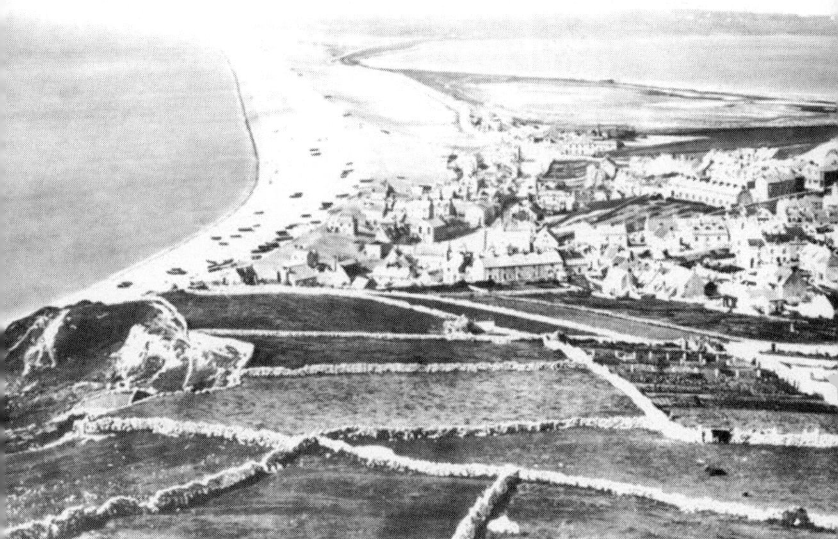

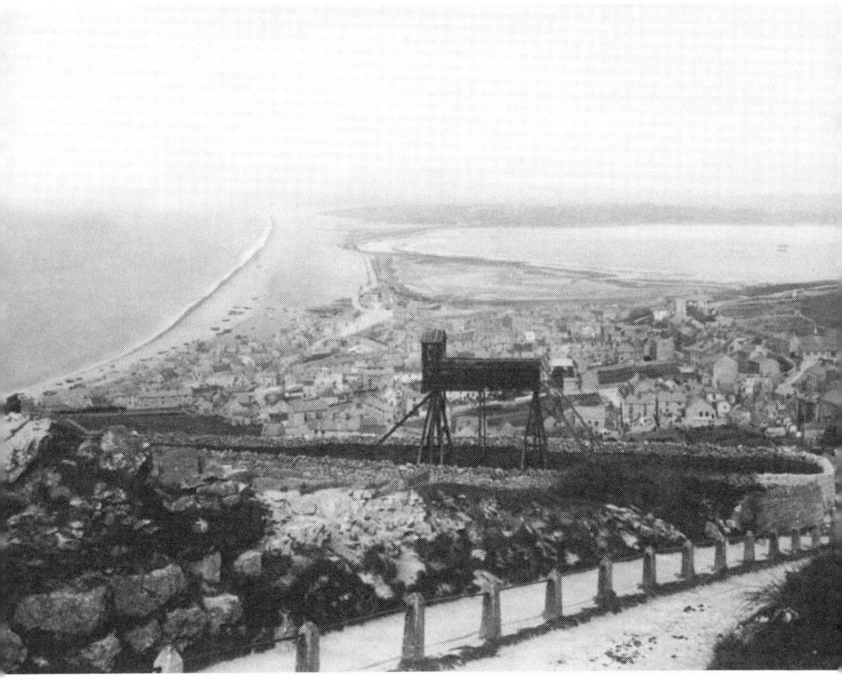

Chesil Beach is a great ridge of shingle eight miles long, with a lagoon of brackish water between it and the mainland. The stones tend to be larger at one end of the beach than the other. John Meade Faulkner immortalised the locality in his famous smuggling novel 'Moonfleet'.

PORTLAND

CHESIL BEACH 1890 / 27328

The great breakwaters around the eastern shores of Portland entirely enclose Portland harbour. They were constructed in the second half of the 19th century to enhance the naval port that had developed over the previous centuries. The older breakwater took twenty-three years to build and cost over a million pounds—a considerable amount of money at that time.

PORTLAND

THE BREAKWATER 1890 / 27333

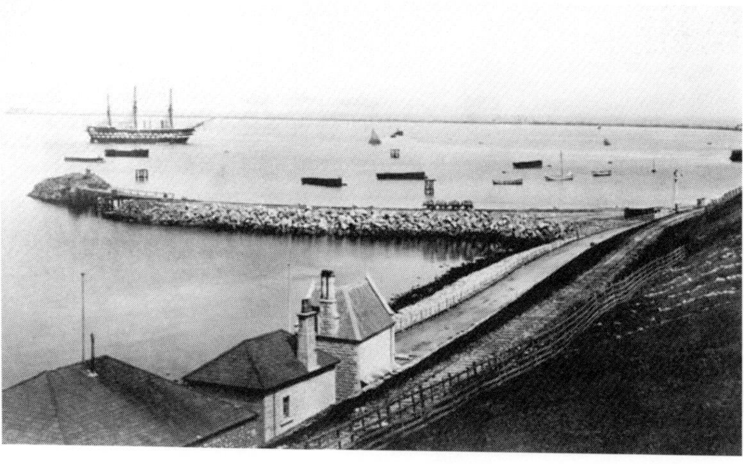

Castletown, Fortuneswell and Chesil now form a large urban settlement where Portland meets the mainland. At the time this photograph was taken, they were three discrete settlements, overlooking the great naval base in one direction and being overlooked by the great convict prison from the other.

PORTLAND

CASTLETOWN FROM CHESIL BEACH 1894 / 34549

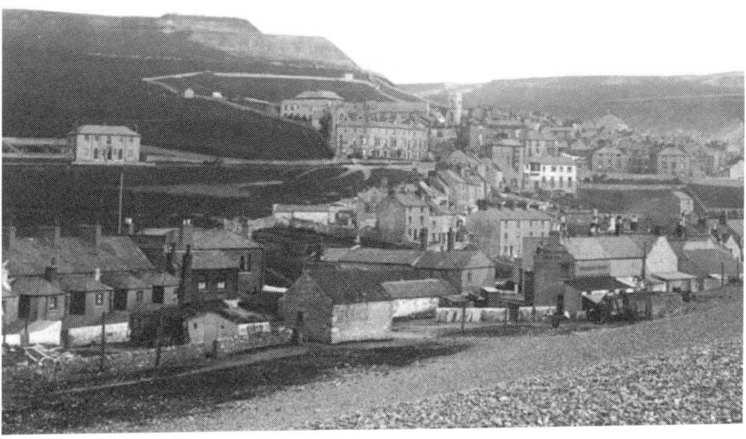

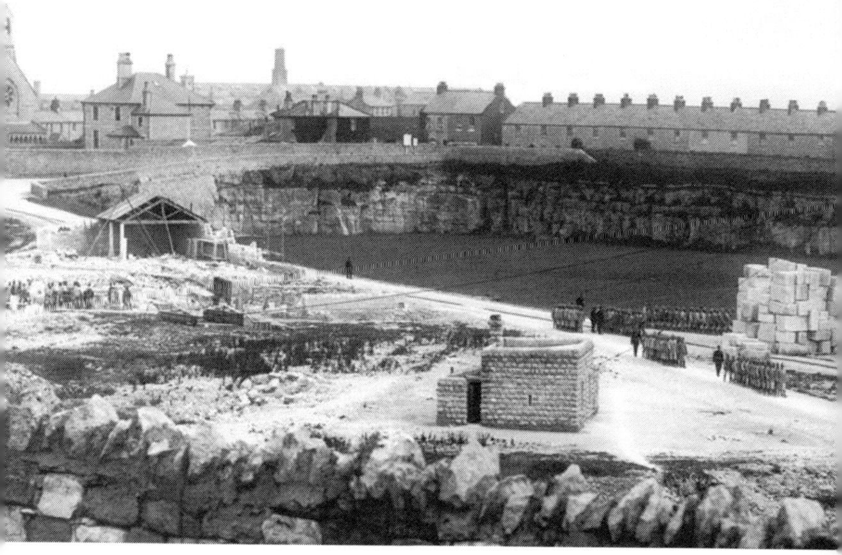

Portland stone is renowned throughout the world as a prime building material. Sir Christopher Wren used this durable material for St. Paul's Cathedral. Apart from private family-run quarries, much of the stone was broken by convicts from the nearby prison. Here we can see convicts being marched in strict order for a day's work with pickaxe and crowbar.

PORTLAND

1894 / 34553

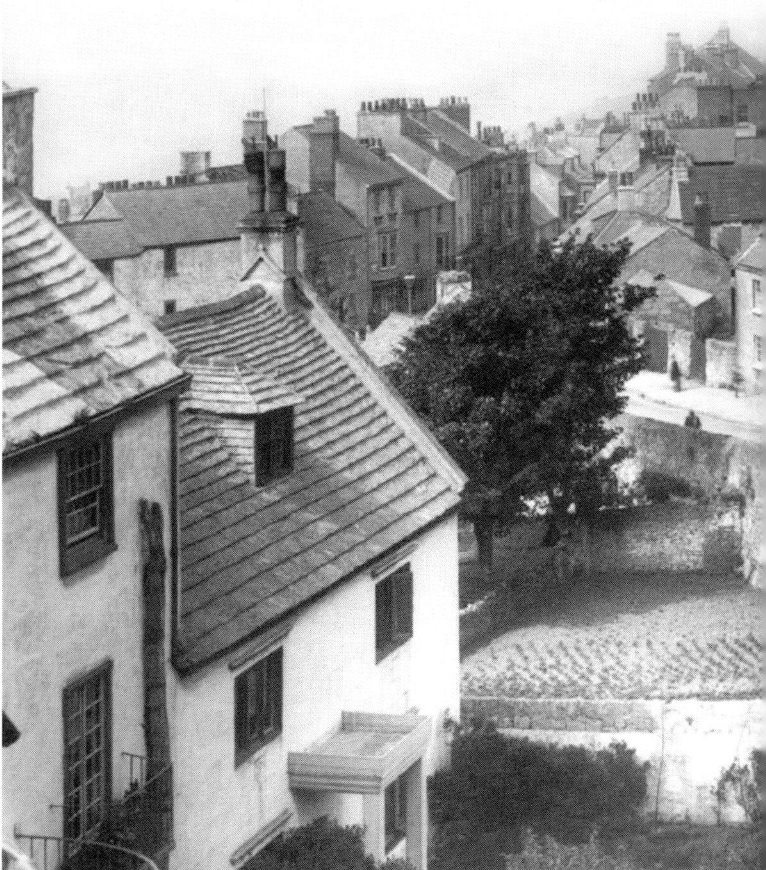

PORTLAND

FORTUNE'S WELL 1894 / 34550

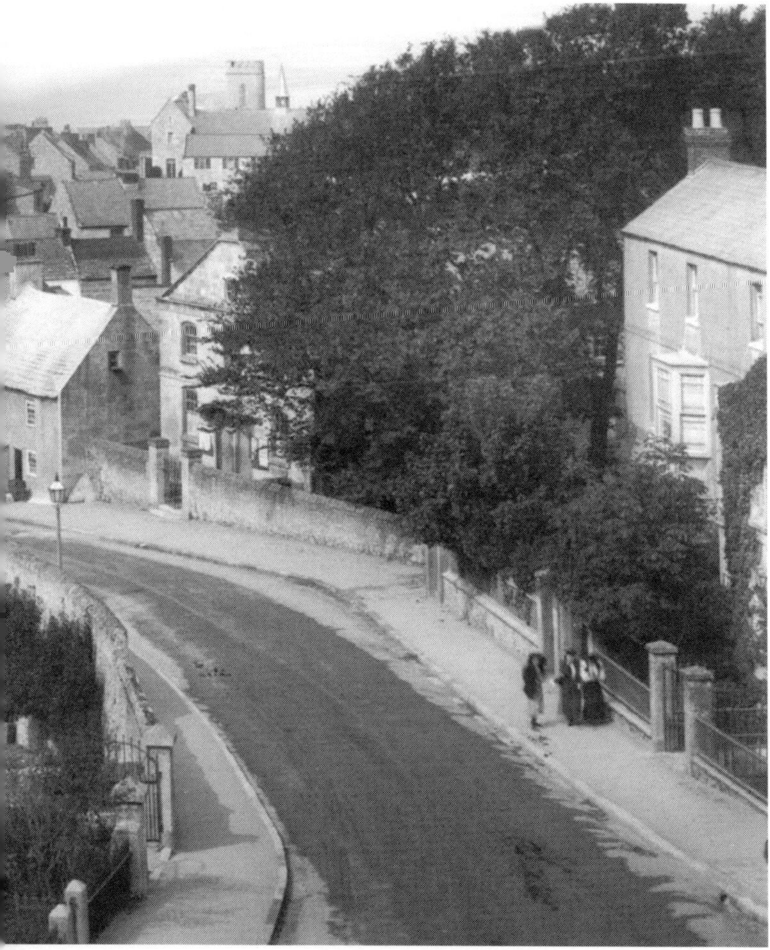

Portland's main town of Fortuneswell grew up, as the name implies, around a well, as did most of the Portland settlements. A supply of pure water would have been essential on this barren rock, almost surrounded by salt water.

Portland Bill juts out into the English Channel at the southernmost point of the island. The Pulpit Rock is just one of the many unusual and dramatic rock formations in the vicinity.

PORTLAND

THE PULPIT ROCK 1898 / 41150

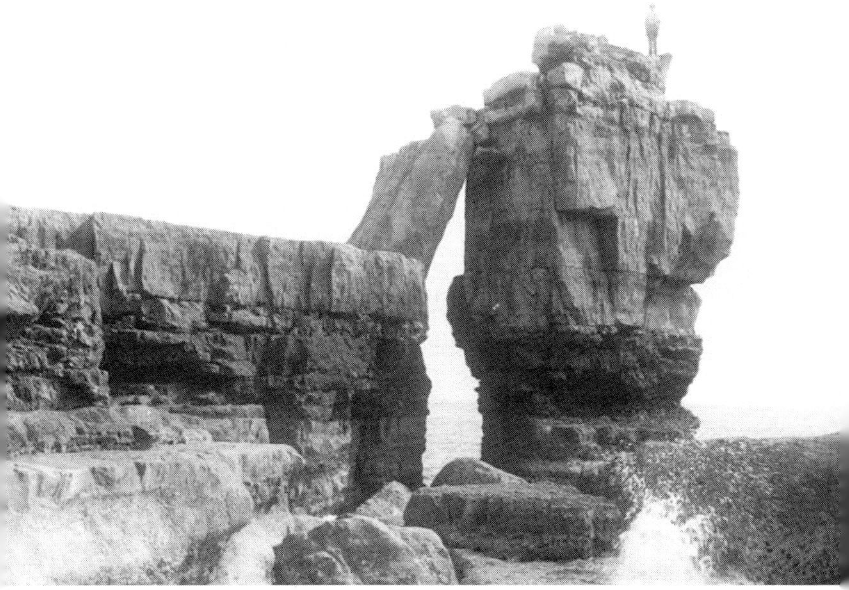

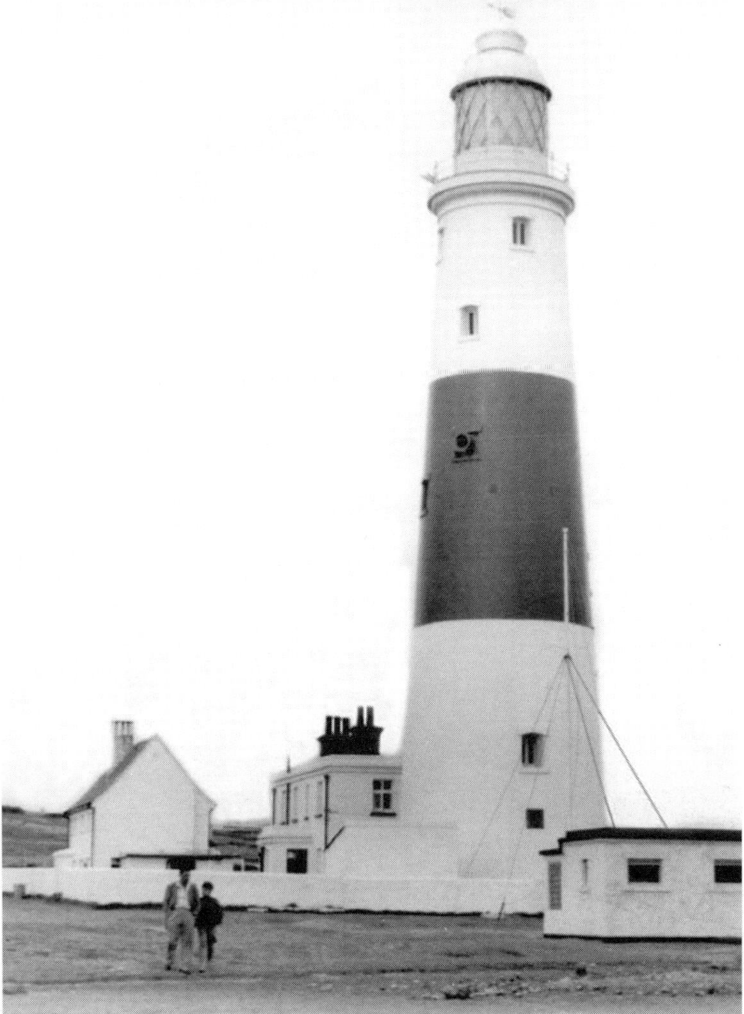

PORTLAND

THE LIGHTHOUSE C1955 / P91022

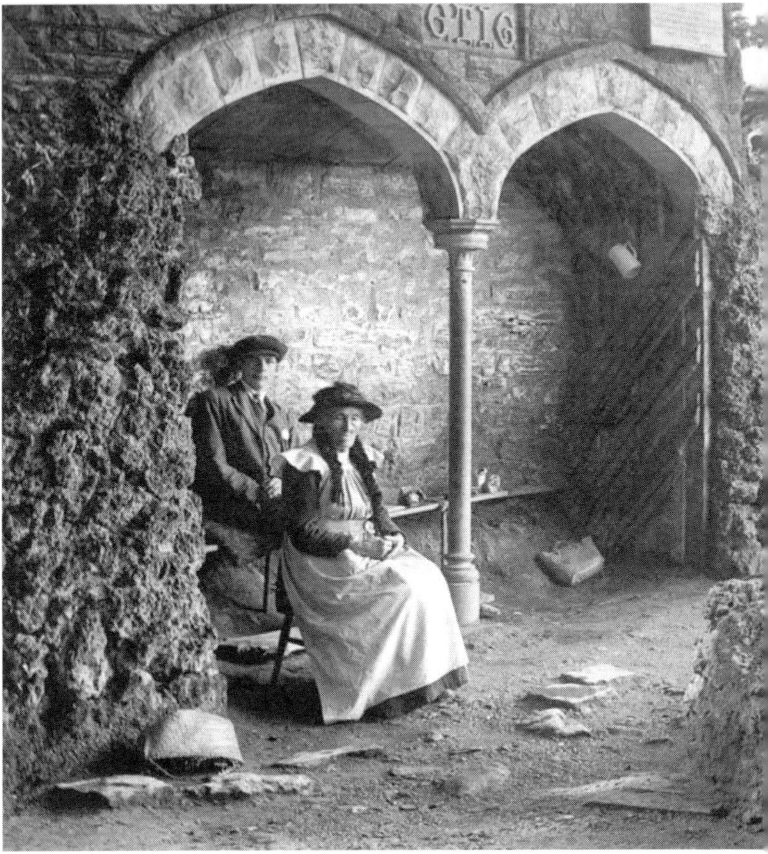

UPWEY

THE WISHING WELL 1923 / 73960

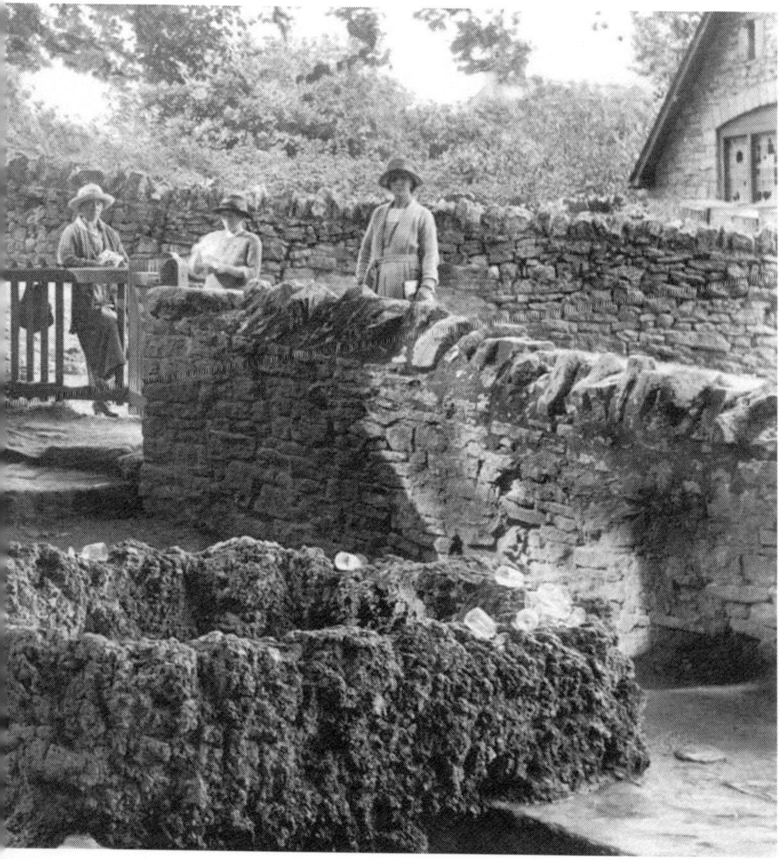

The village of Upwey stands on the high road between Weymouth and Dorchester and features in Thomas Hardy's novel 'The Trumpet-Major'. The famous wishing well was a favourite day out for early visitors to Weymouth, who would taste the water and think of their heart's desire. A shack nearby provided simple refreshments, and the tourists would sit on the surrounding benches.

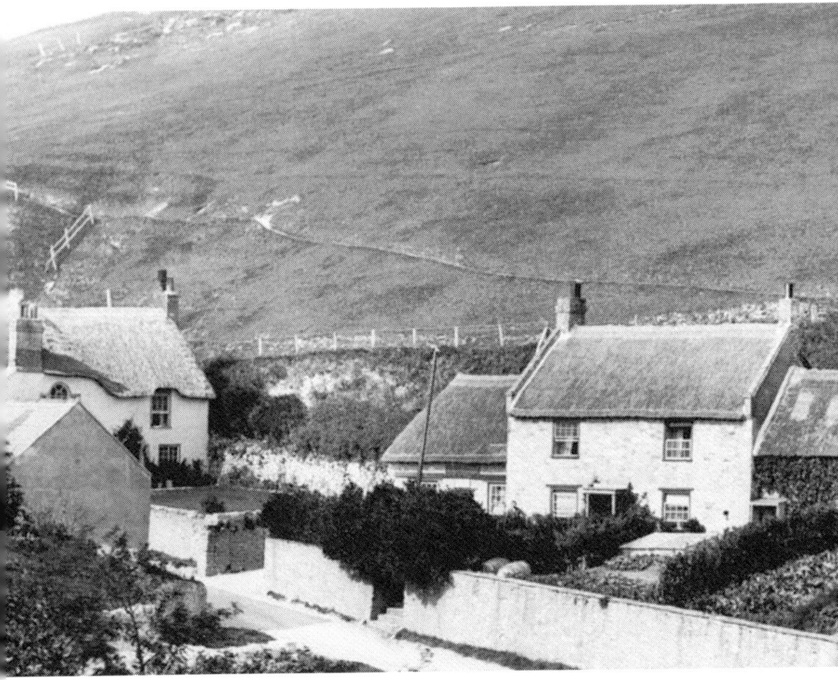

The villages of West and East Lulworth now stand adjacent to vast military firing ranges, though fortunately they never suffered the fate of nearby Tyneham, which was taken by the army during the Second World War and never returned to its villagers.

LULWORTH

BISHOP'S COTTAGE 1894 / 34563

A perfect natural harbour, Lulworth Cove has been hollowed out by the swirling waters of the English Channel into its present almost circular form, creating one of the most distinctive bays on the coast of southern England.

LULWORTH COVE

WEST POINT 1894 / 34575

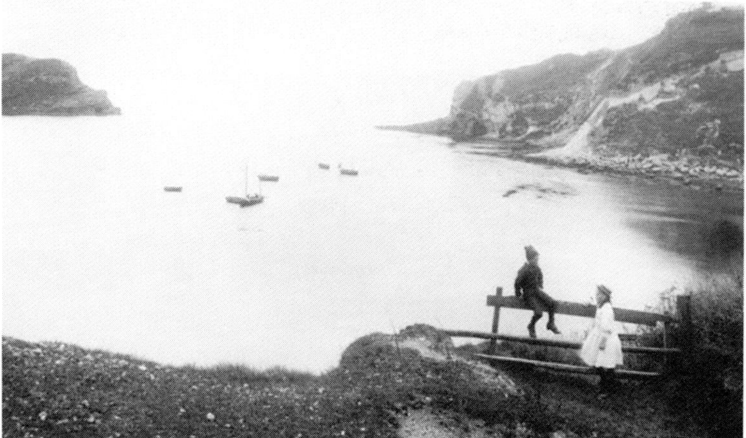

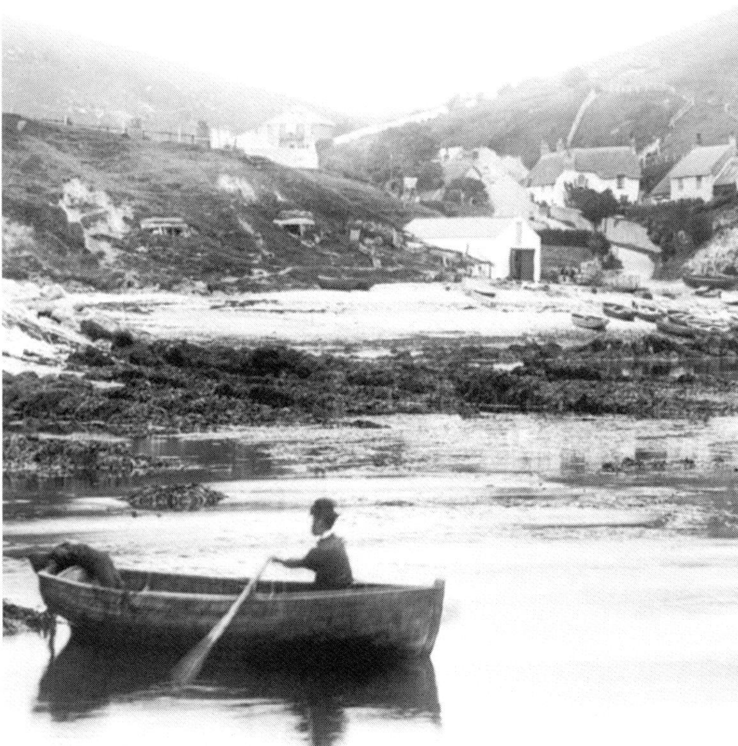

LULWORTH COVE

1894 / 34569

We are looking towards Stair Hole, where the downlands of Dorset meet the sea, is hollowed out by vast caverns, many used by smugglers for centuries. The South West Way Coastal Footpath, once an old coastguard route, gives excellent views over these wild headlands and coves. The beauty of Lulworth Cove has always attracted writers and artists. John Keats spent some of his last days in England here, and Thomas Hardy immortalised the cove in poems and novels.

LULWORTH COVE

1903 / 49137

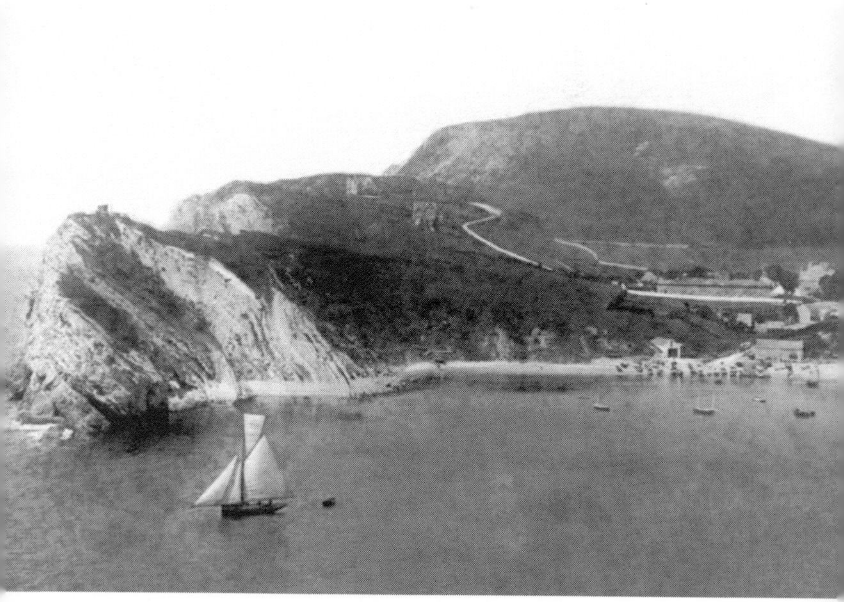

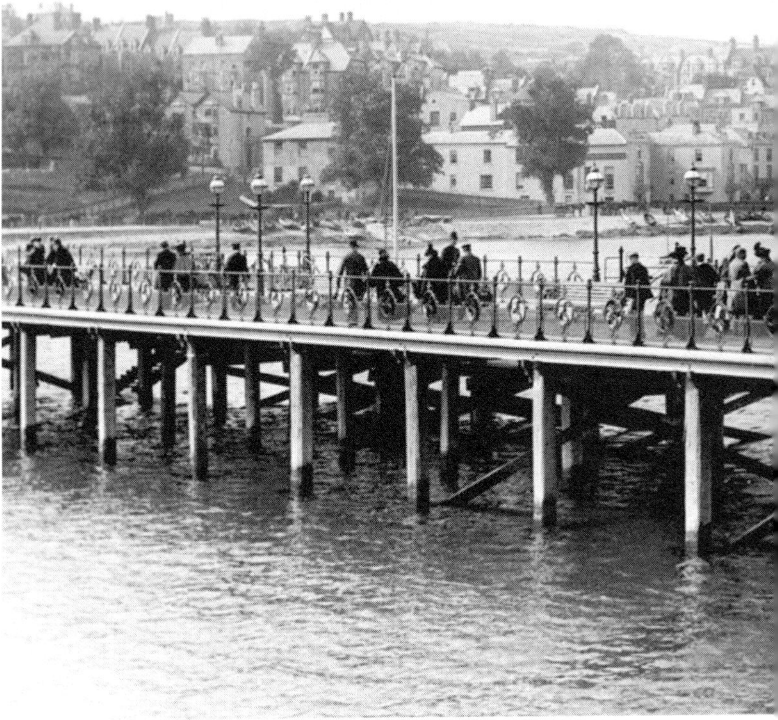

SWANAGE

FROM THE PIER 1897 / 40301

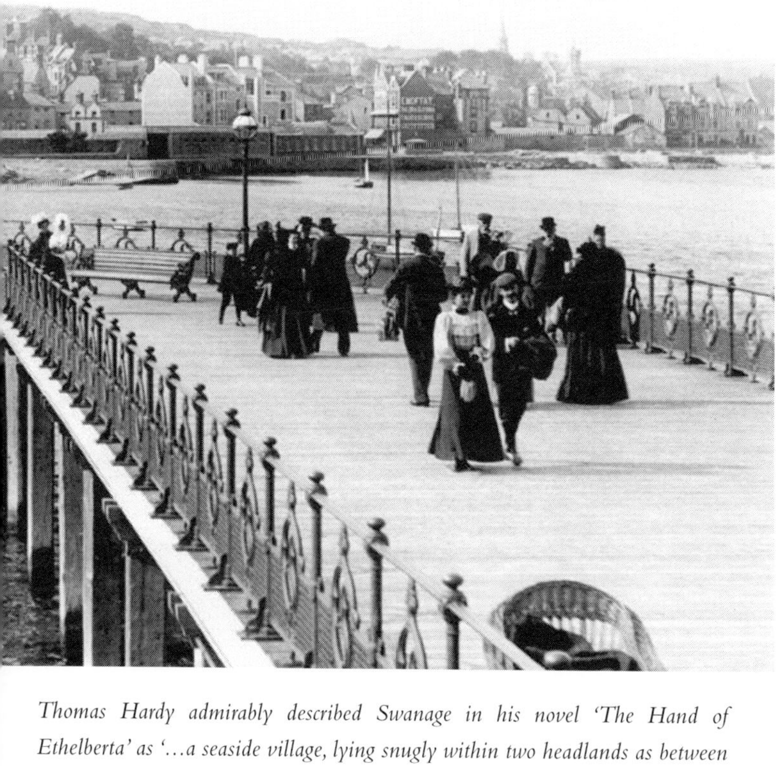

Thomas Hardy admirably described Swanage in his novel 'The Hand of Ethelberta' as '...a seaside village, lying snugly within two headlands as between a finger and thumb.' Swanage Pier is really a jetty, 28 feet wide and 1,400 feet long. When this photograph was taken, the pier would have been mostly used to give access to the great number of coastal steamers that anchored alongside each day to carry passengers to towns like Weymouth and Bournemouth.

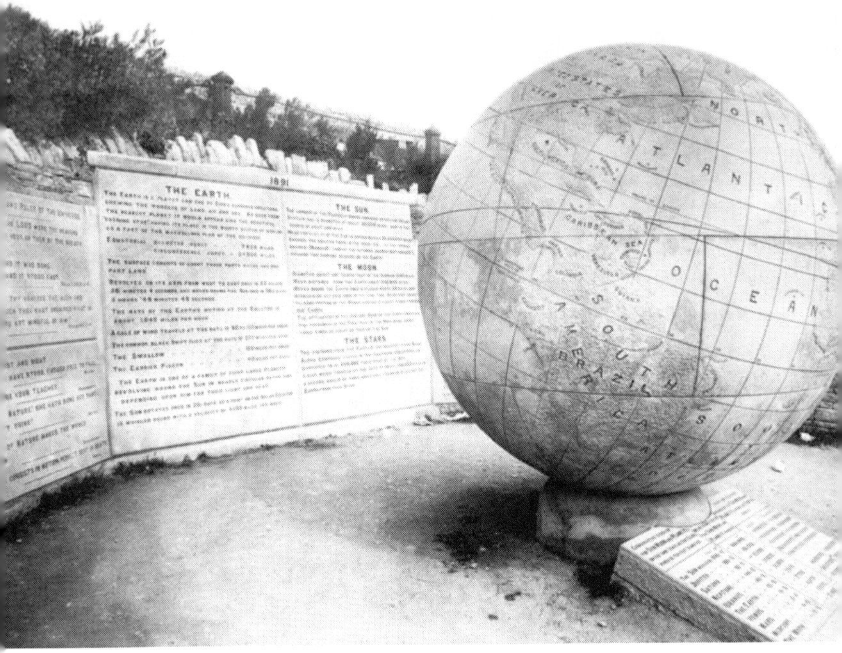

The Globe at Swanage was carved out of a great mass of Portland Stone, ten feet in diameter and forty tons in weight. The Globe is positioned to represent the position of the earth in space, with nearby benches marking the points of the compass. The Isle of Purbeck, that great peninsula sprawling eastwards into Poole harbour, is riddled with quarries. The railway station at Swanage was used to bring the stone to ships for transportation around the world.

SWANAGE

THE GLOBE 1894 / 34607

Swanage may get its name from Swene's Wic, the Bay of Swene, perhaps commemorating the naval battle between Saxons and Danes in 877. The Isle of Purbeck was a great stronghold for the Wessex Saxons for three centuries.

SWANAGE

FROM THE COASTGUARD STATION 1897 / 40308

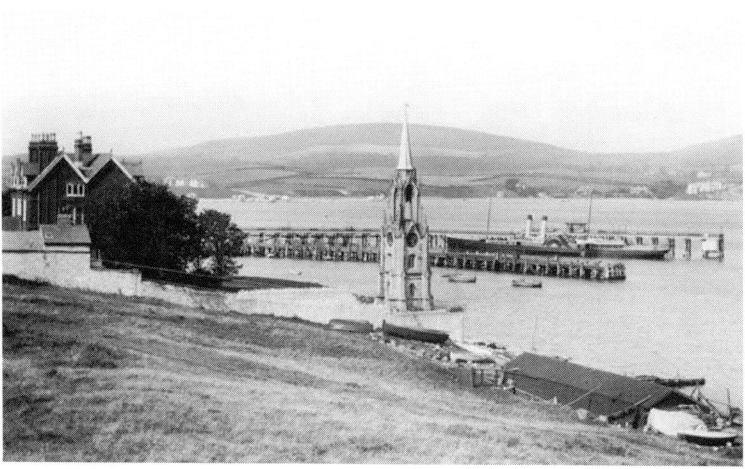

For hundreds of years, the nearness of Purbeck to the coast of France meant that smuggling was a major industry; smuggled goods would often be hidden in the caves and quarries of the Isle. Prominent coastguard stations with clear Channel views were built along the coast as a deterrent, such as this one at Swanage. Coastal watching also helped to safeguard small boats caught out in wild water and uncertain tides.

SWANAGE

THE COASTGUARD STATION 1897 / 40310

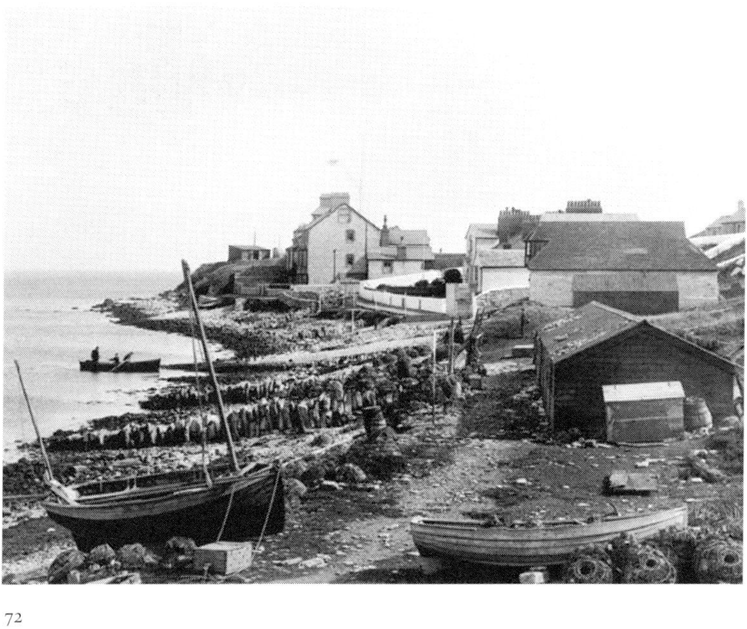

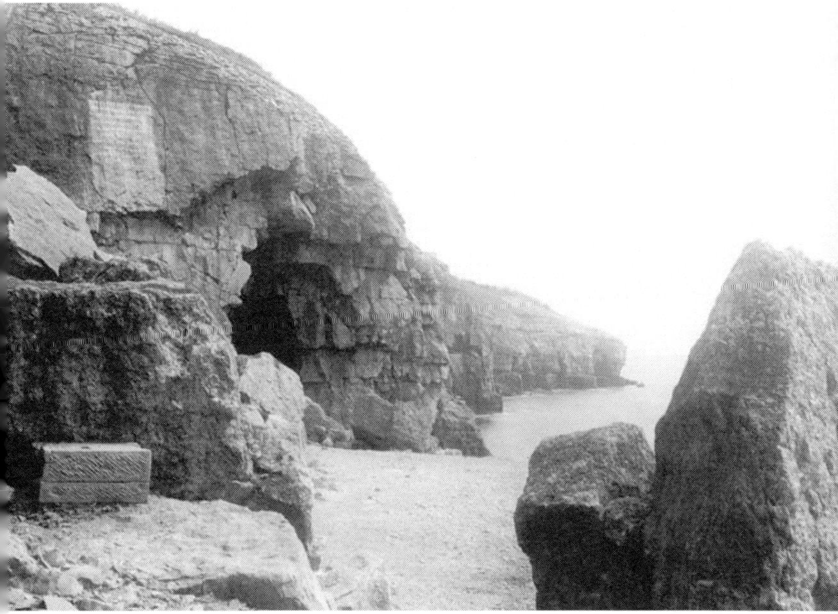

Tilly Whim Caves, on the coast west of Swanage, are a strange mixture of natural erosion and quarrying. Tilly Whim was an attraction noted by early guidebook writers, who nevertheless deplored the graffiti carved into the rocks by Victorian visitors.

SWANAGE

TILLY WHIM 1899 / 43775

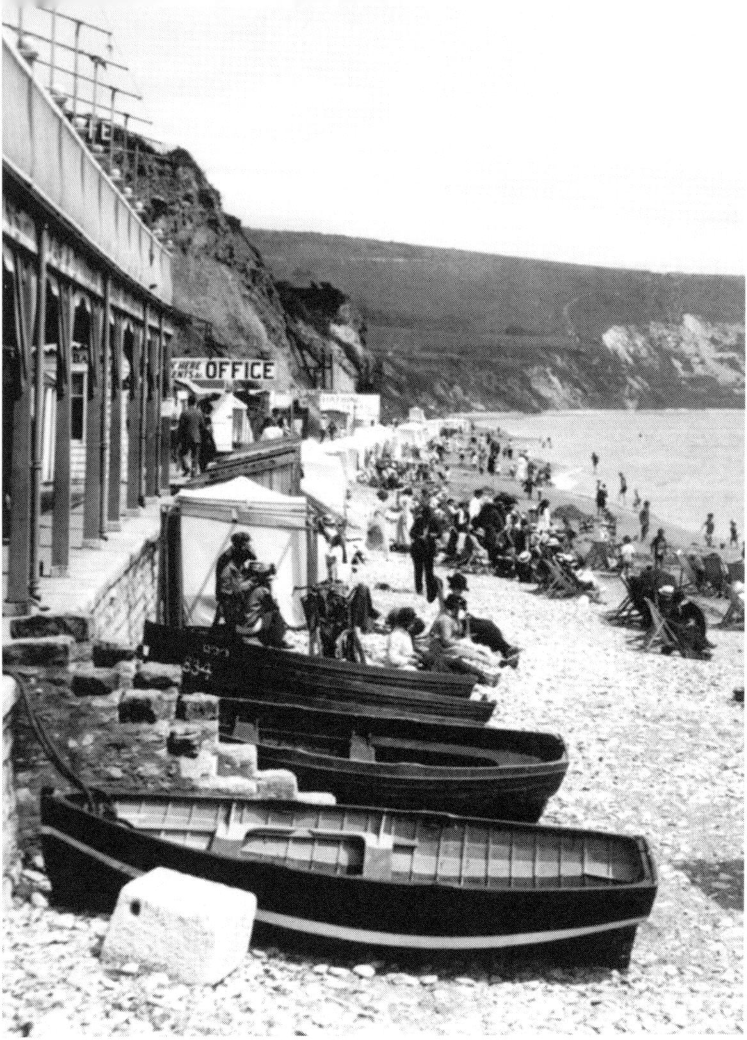

SWANAGE

THE BEACH 1918 / 68090

On Swanage's mixed bathing beach tents were provided for changing and preserving the modesty of visitors. Men were charged three old pence and ladies four old pence for the privilege of using the facilities, though bathers could pitch their own tent for two shillings and sixpence (15 pence) a week.

SWANAGE

THE PROMENADE 1925 / 78791

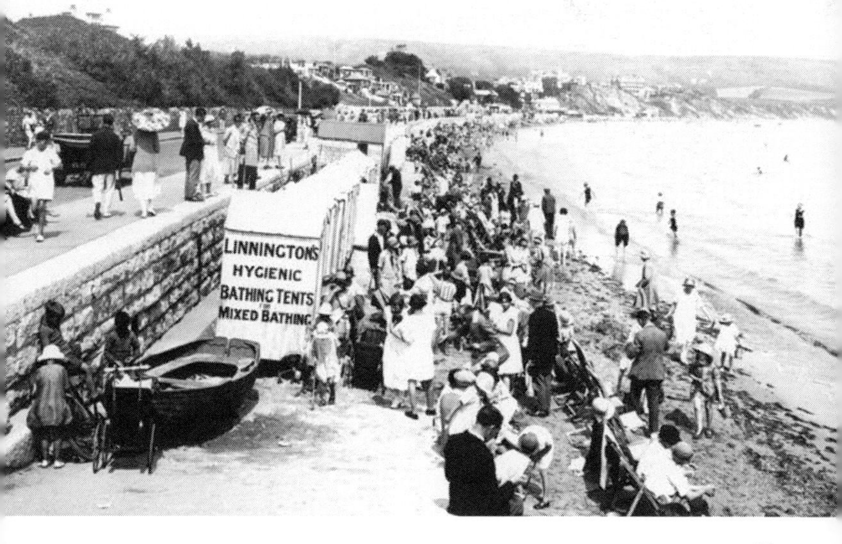

Station Road was probably the first view of the town for most tourists, leading as it does from the railway to the sea front. It was a popular street for local shoppers, with a large selection of family retailers, though even as long ago as 1925 shops were catering for tourists with beach goods and souvenirs.

SWANAGE

STATION ROAD 1925 / 78794

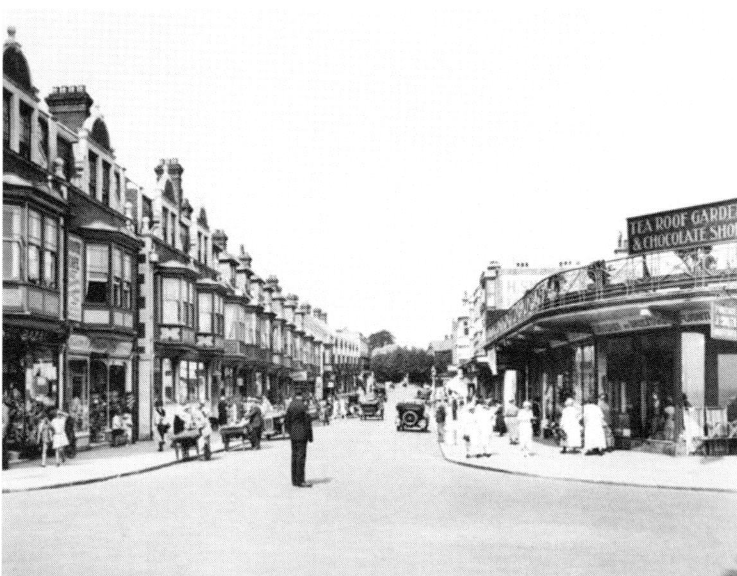

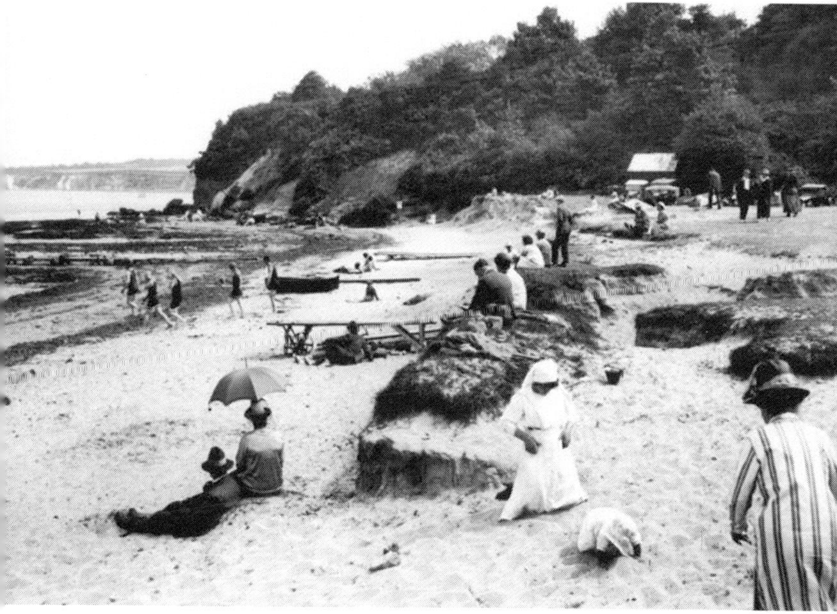

The journey to Studland Bay was probably the favourite excursion for tourists from Swanage, who could either get there by walking along the cliff tops or by taking a carriage or charabanc along the lanes, admiring the views across to Bournemouth, the Needles and the Isle of Wight as they went. The attraction of Studland is not only the splendid beach and picturesque coastal scenery, but also the wild heathland all around the village.

STUDLAND

THE BEACH 1925 / 78796

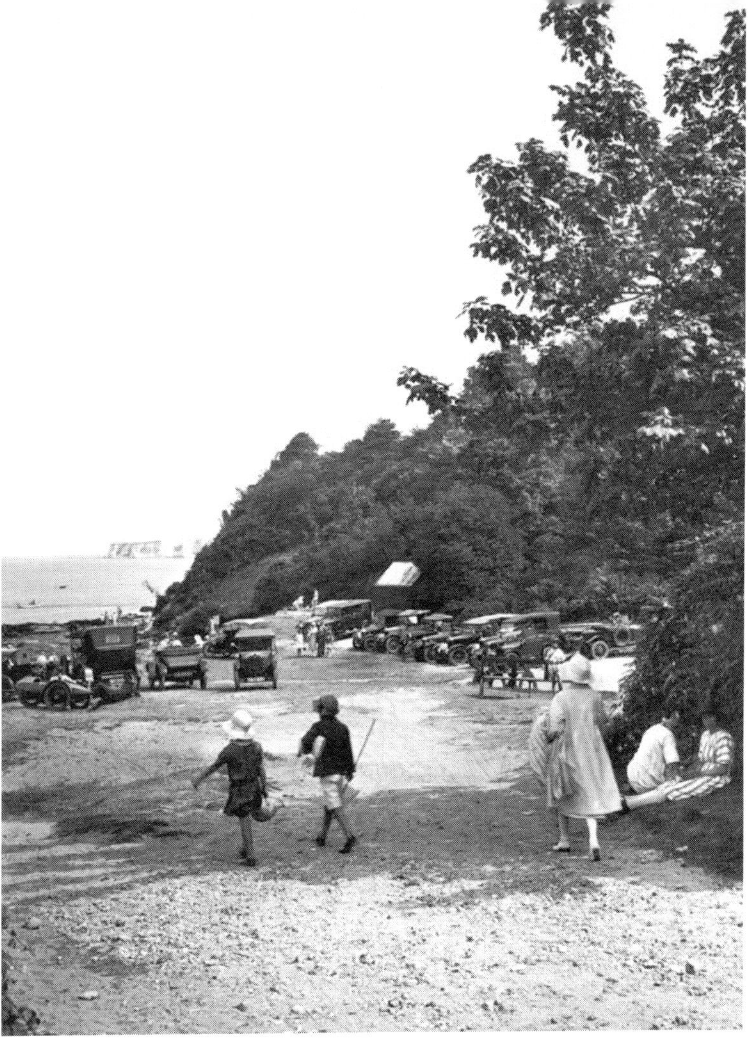

STUDLAND

THE BEACH 1925 / 78797

The town of Poole grew up around the older quays of the great harbour; during these times it was purely functional, catering for mercantile activities, shipping and pottery manufactured from the local clays. Poole is still an important port, though more now the haunt of leisure craft than merchant shipping.

POOLE

THE HARBOUR 1900 / 46089

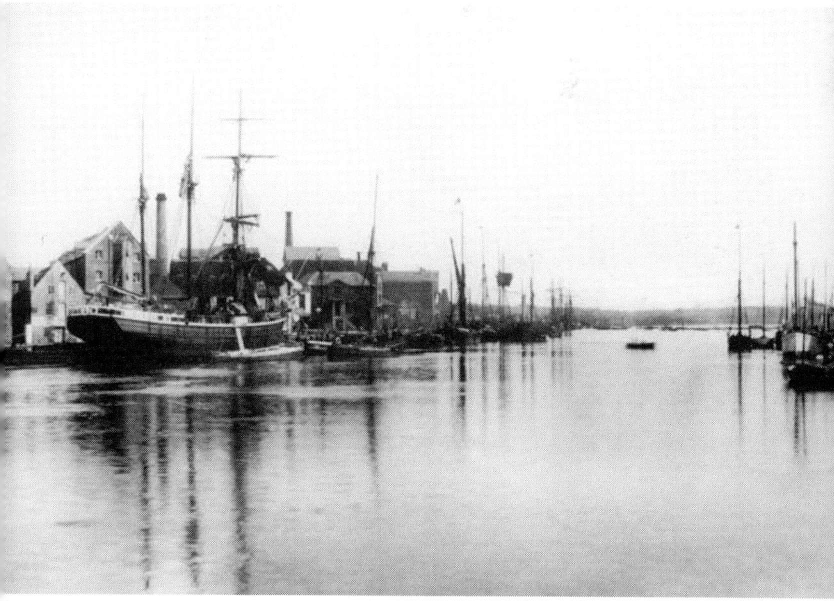

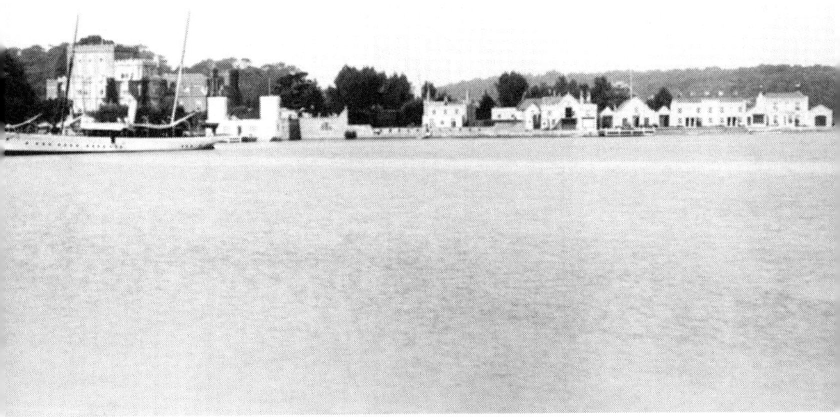

Brownsea is the largest island in Poole Harbour and now belongs to the National Trust. In 1907, Robert Baden Powell held a camp for boys on the island, which laid the foundations for the Boy Scout movement, which he initiated not long afterwards.

BROWNSEA ISLAND

THE CASTLE 1904 / 52801

Close to the quays at Poole is the 18th-century Harbour Office, once the Old Town House, a club for ships captains. On the front of the building is an old sundial, and on the side a carving of Benjamin Skutt, who was Mayor of Poole in 1727.

POOLE

THE HARBOUR OFFICE 1904 / 52815

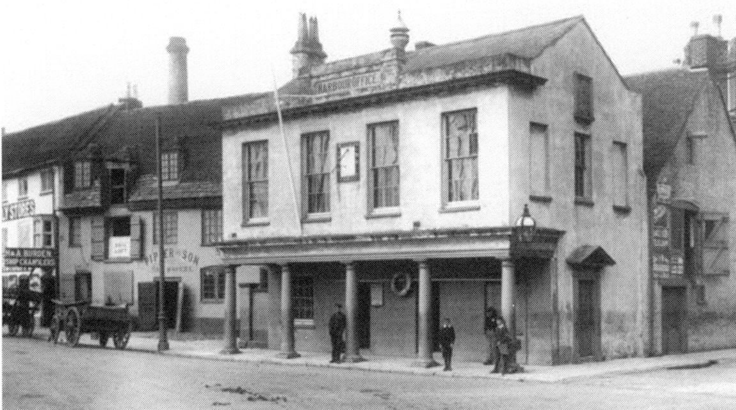

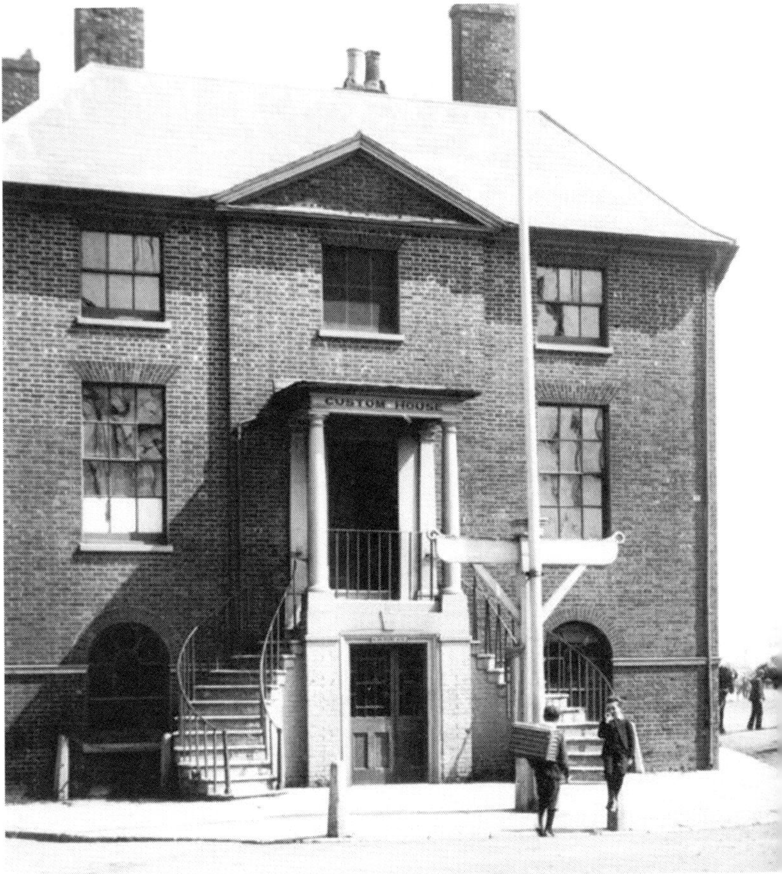

POOLE

THE CUSTOM HOUSE 1904 / 52814

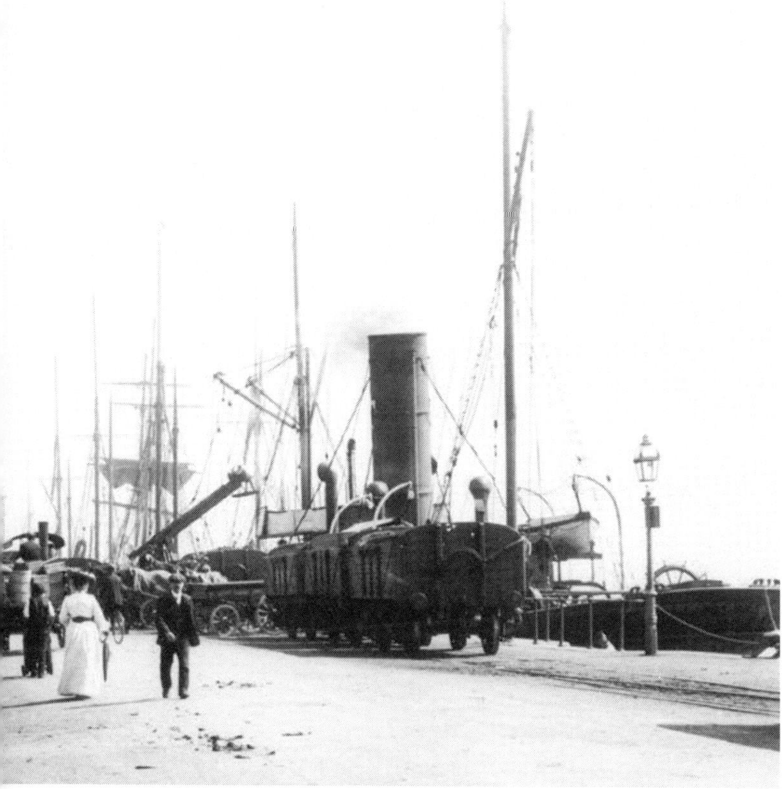

In 1747 a valuable cargo of tea was seized by the revenue men and stored in the old Custom House at Poole. A band of well-armed smugglers attacked the Custom House in retaliation, seizing the tea and putting the revenue men to flight. The tea mysteriously disappeared inland on the back of a procession of packhorses.

The cellars are situated in one of the oldest parts of town; we see it here on a busy day at the height of Poole's mercantile past. Poole had many independent breweries at this time; here we see one of their horse drawn drays on a delivery round.

POOLE

THE TOWN CELLARS 1887 / 19511

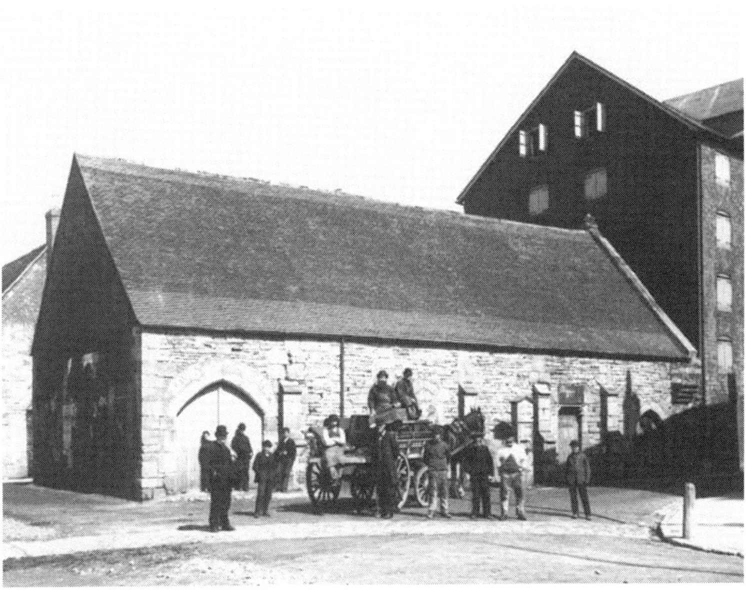

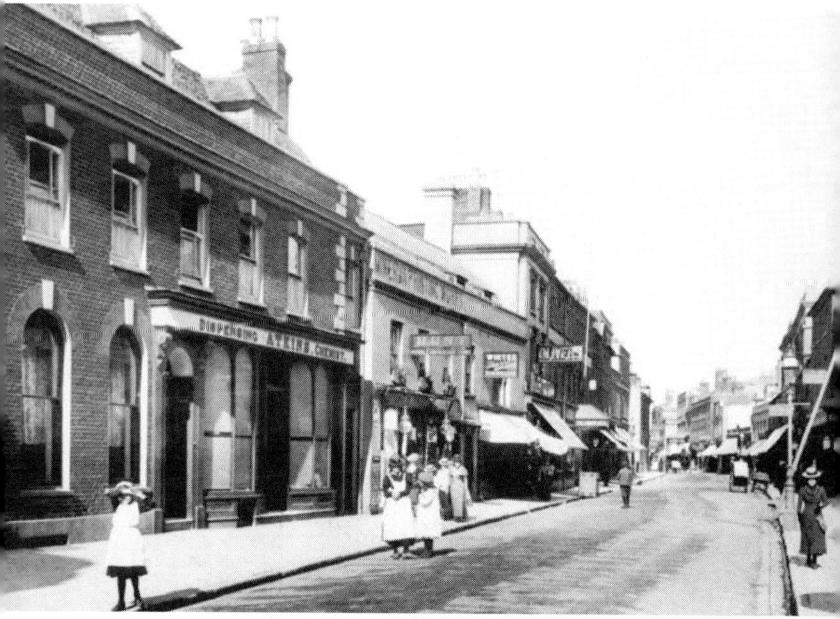

Poole developed along the banks of the finest natural harbour in England. It still maintains strong links with the sea, having become a mecca for yachtsmen. The prosperous town, built where the sea meets the wild heathlands of Dorset, is one of the largest along the south coast. Although spoiled by modern development, the tangle of streets around the old town is worth exploring and there is still much fine Georgian and Victorian architecture to be seen.

POOLE

HIGH STREET 1900 / 46087

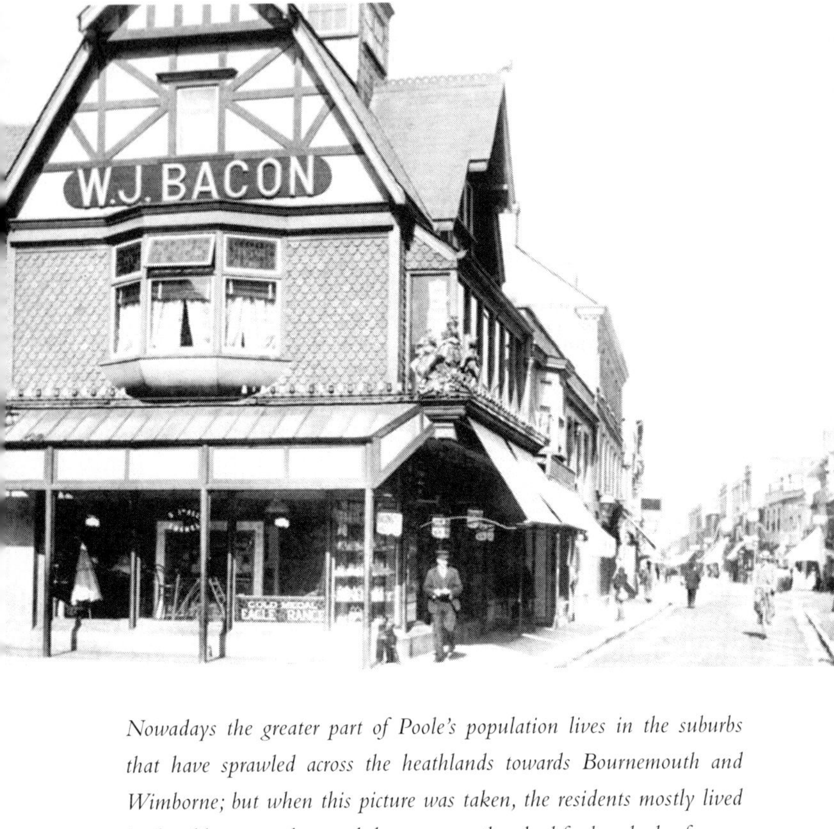

Nowadays the greater part of Poole's population lives in the suburbs that have sprawled across the heathlands towards Bournemouth and Wimborne; but when this picture was taken, the residents mostly lived in the old town and around the quays, as they had for hundreds of years.

POOLE

HIGH STREET 1900 / 46088

Trams were an efficient form of transport, which lasted for a great many years in Poole. They harnessed the power of the newly-introduced electricity as the driving force, as we can see from the power lines above. Cyclists and pedestrians occasionally found the tram-lines an extra hazard on Dorset's rough and ready roads.

POOLE

LONGFLEET ROAD 1904 / 52811

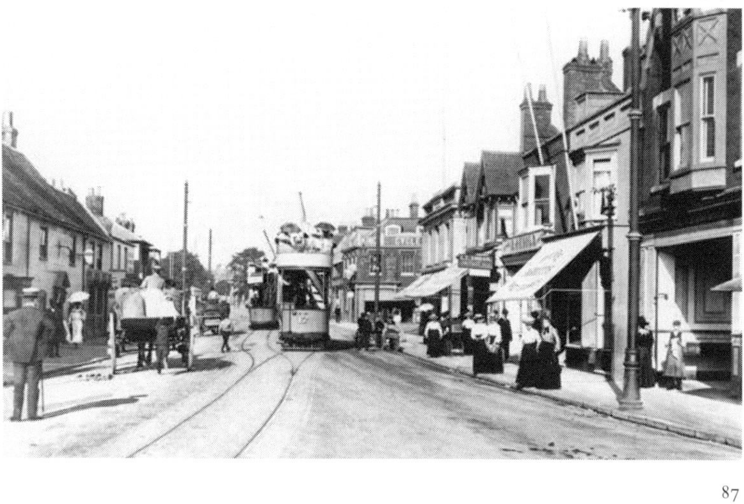

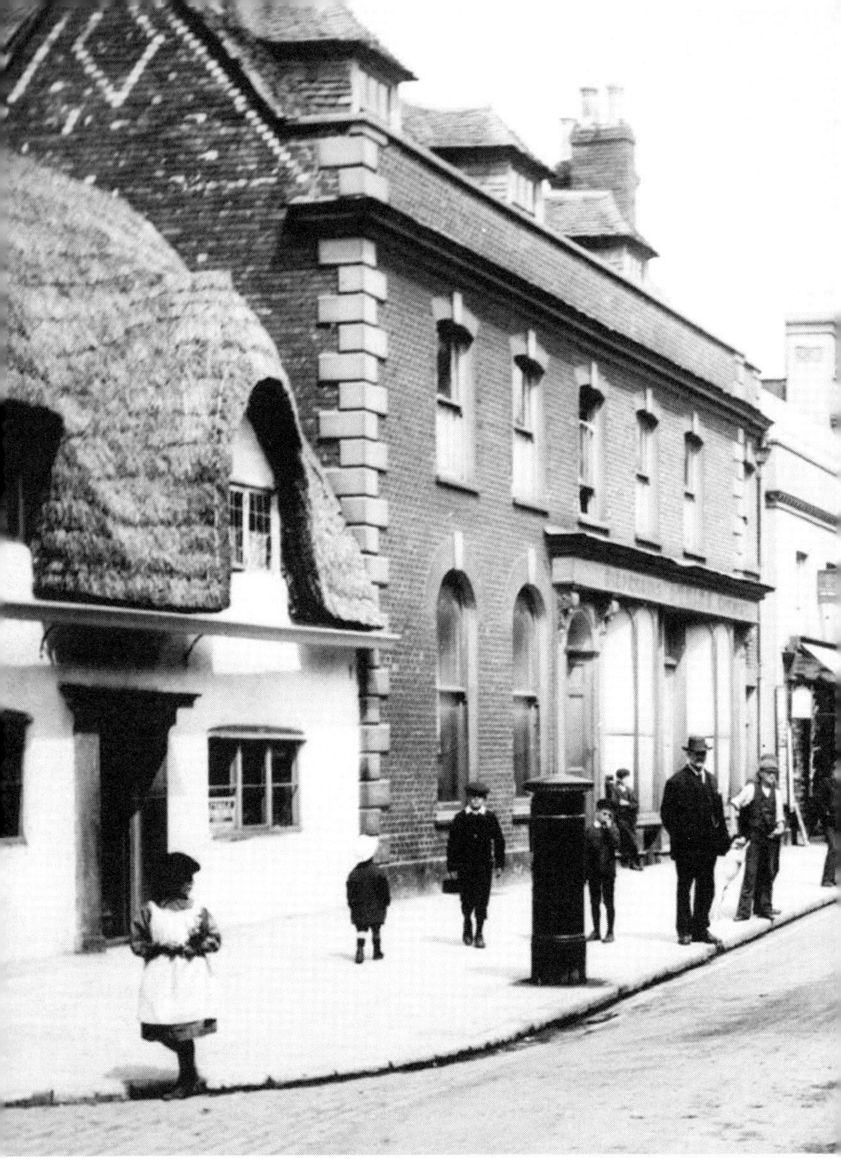

POOLE

HIGH STREET 1908 / 61164

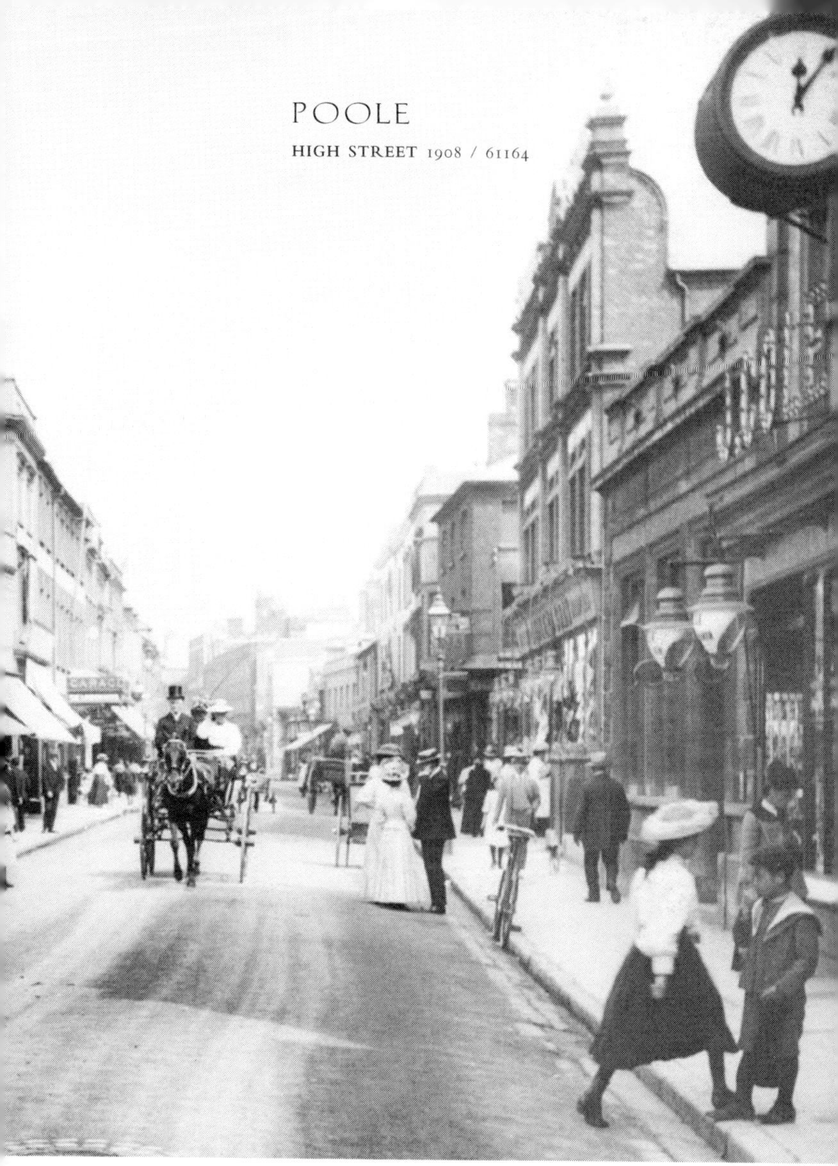

With its fine views across the harbour, Poole Park became a popular gathering ground for tourists who wanted to walk, row boats or just sit in the sunshine.

POOLE

THE PARK 1904 / 52802

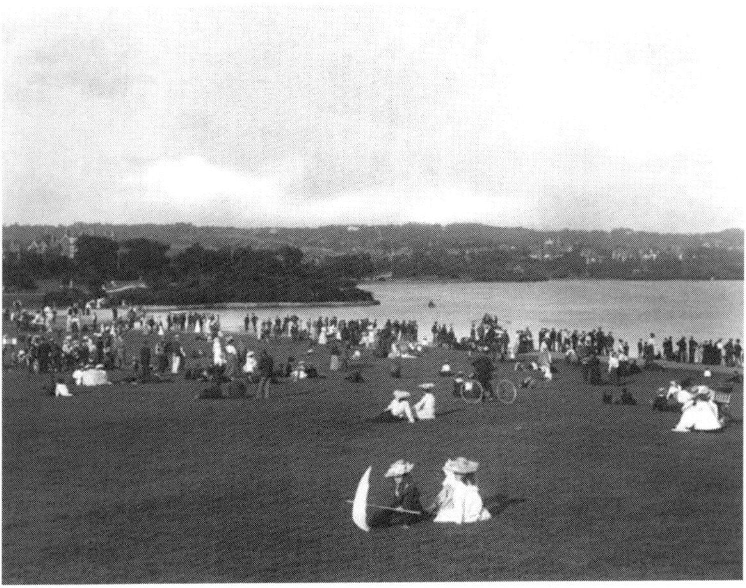

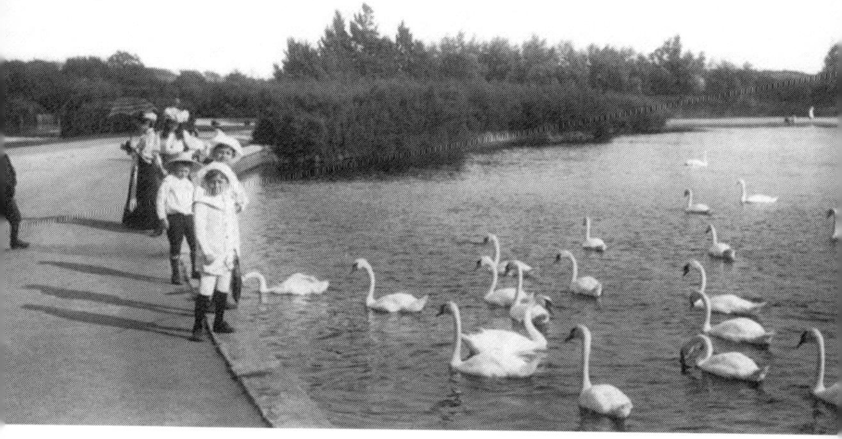

In 1890 the Prince of Wales opened Poole Park, once a forbidding swamp on the edge of the harbour, on land donated by Lord Wimborne. The park lake covers some 60 acres and serves for boating and as a sanctuary for tamer wildfowl.

POOLE

PARK LAKE 1908 / 61176

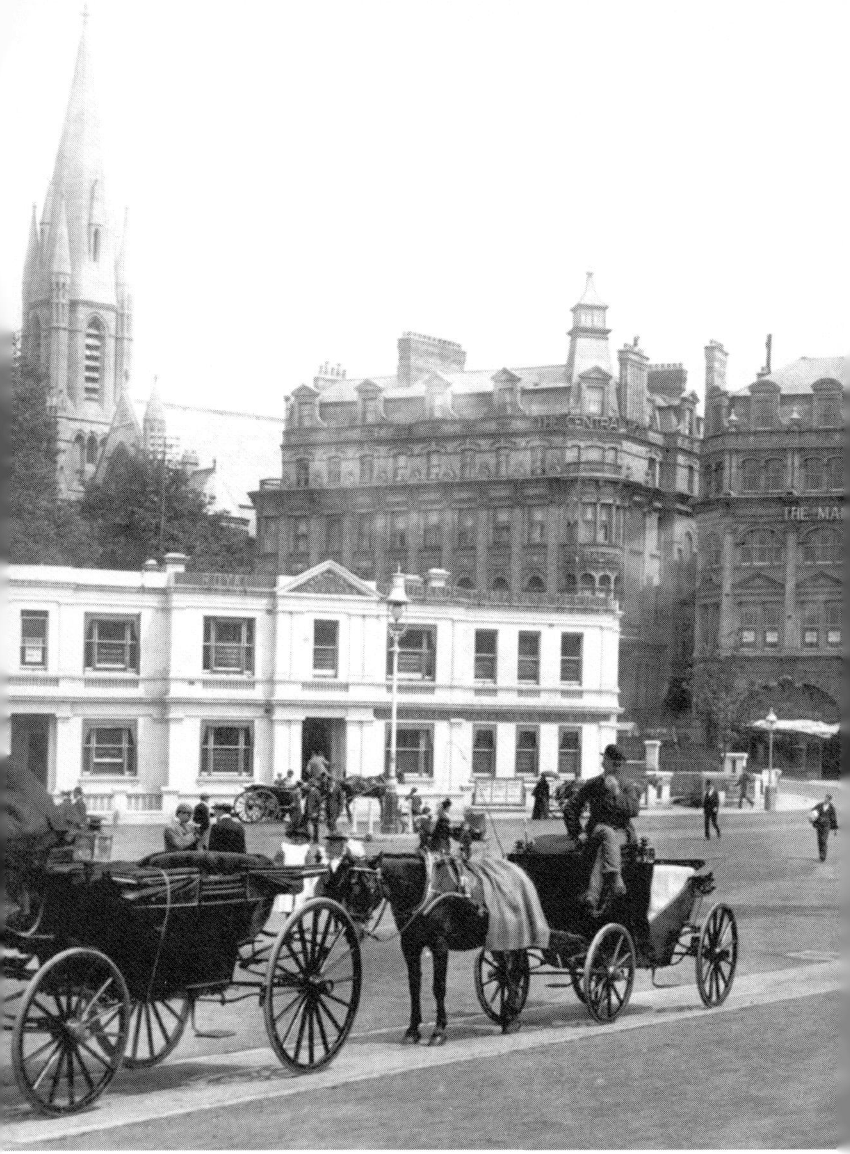

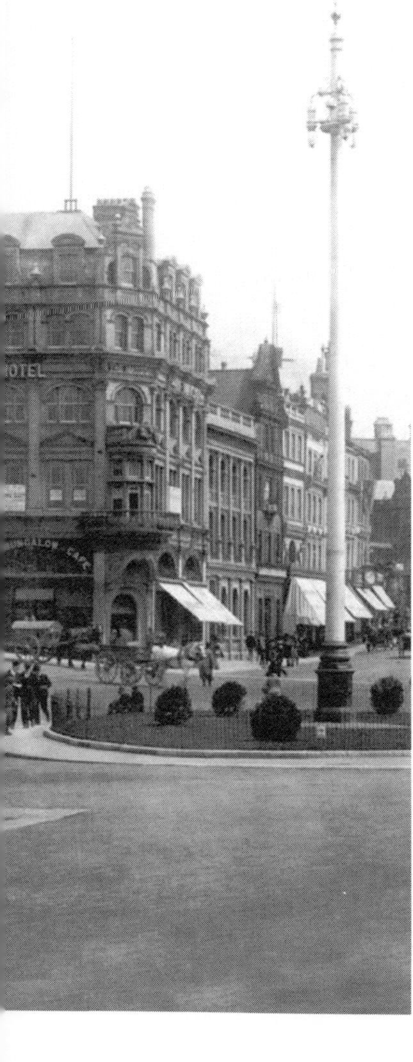

Like so many seaside resorts of the 19th century, Bournemouth attracted a wealthy clientele who built villas for semi-permanent and permanent occupation. The prestigious shopping streets in the background quickly grew up to cater for their many needs. Here we see horse-drawn cabs waiting for passengers in the Square.

BOURNEMOUTH

THE SQUARE 1900 / 45218

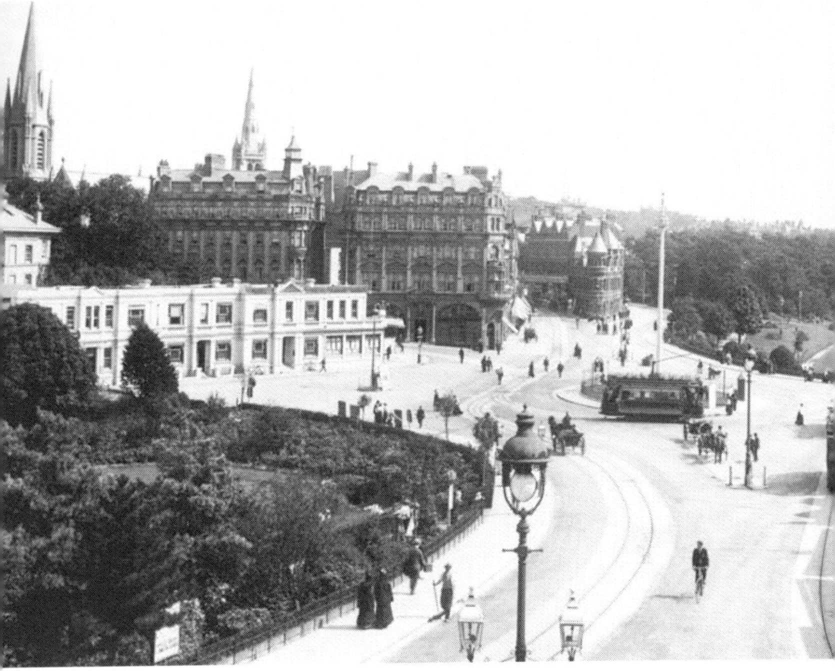

The Square stands at the very heart of the town, astride the River Bourne. Since its early days as a resort, Bournemouth has striven to be the 'garden city by the sea', and its lovely flower displays are a famous attraction for visitors.

BOURNEMOUTH

THE SQUARE 1904 / 52874

Bournemouth, once in Hampshire but now in Dorset, did not exist two hundred years ago. In 1810, Lewis Tregonwell built a house on lonely heathland close to the mouth of the River Bourne. During the years that followed other wealthy Hampshire gentlemen followed his example. It was to be the very end of the century before the town became popular as a holiday resort.

BOURNEMOUTH

THE GARDENS 1904 / 52877

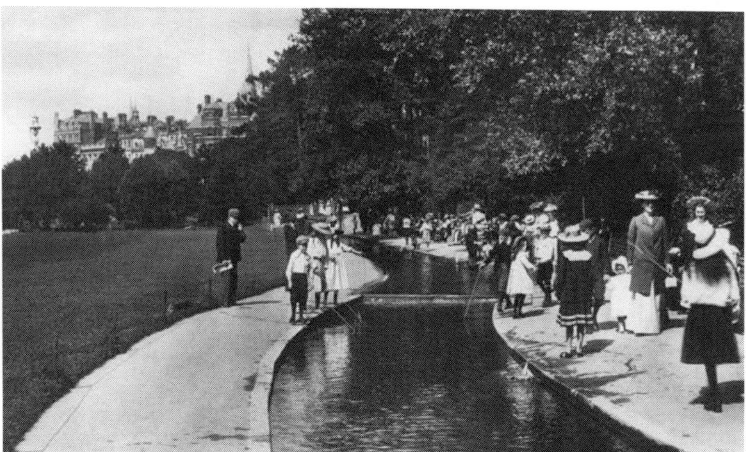

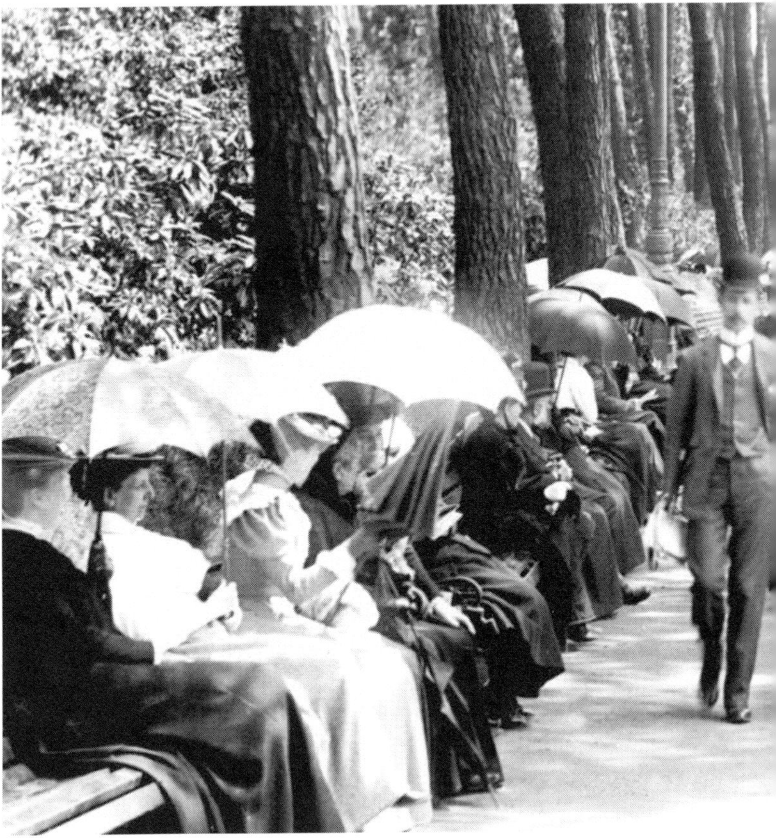

BOURNEMOUTH

INVALIDS' WALK 1900 / 45226

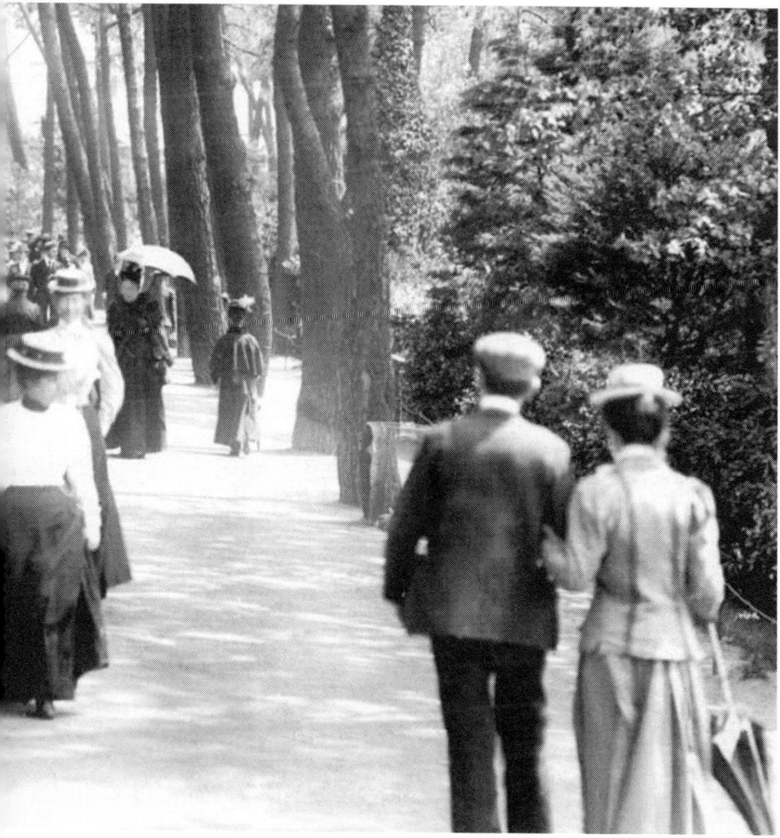

Bournemouth became a sanctuary for the rich and famous. Mary Shelley, creator of Frankenstein, lived here for many years and is buried in the town alongside the heart of her poet husband. Robert Louis Stevenson came to the coast here to benefit his health, and wrote 'Kidnapped' while in the town. Another famous visitor was King Edward VII, who discreetly entertained his mistress Lilly Langtry nearby.

By the 1950s, Bournemouth was at the height of its popularity and one of the most prosperous towns in England, as this view of the town centre shows. At the height of the summer it became difficult to find an available bed in the resort's many hotels and guest houses. In the background here is the 200-foot high spire of St. Peter's church, which dominates the heart of Bournemouth.

BOURNEMOUTH

TOWN CENTRE C1955 / B163109

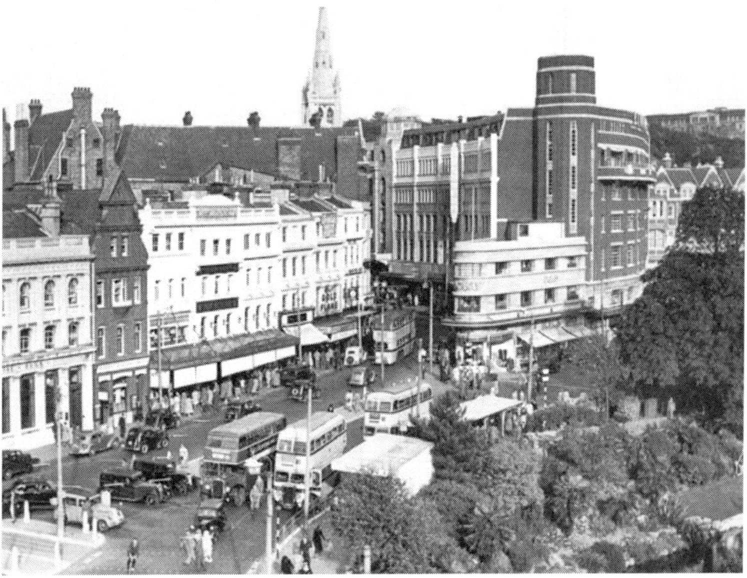

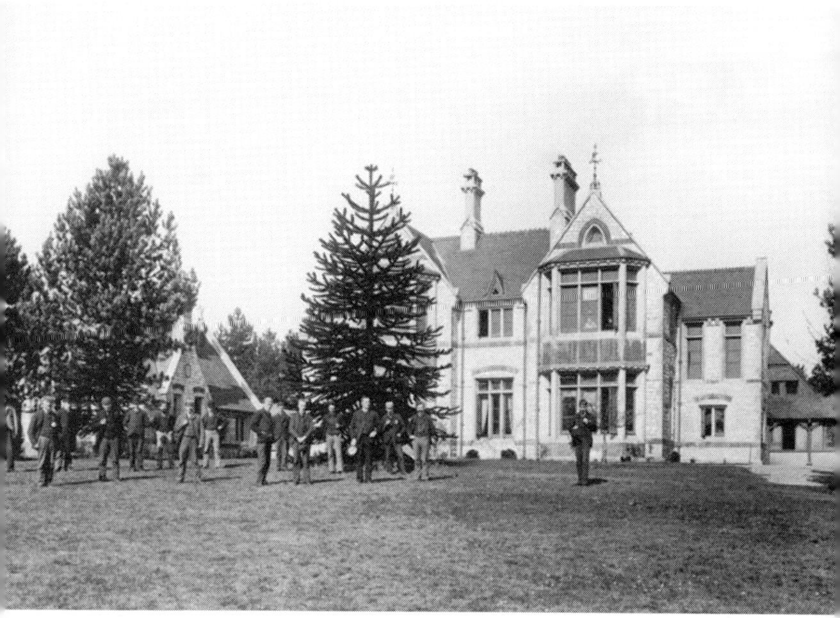

Westbourne, on the west side of Bournemouth, retains a village atmosphere even today, with spacious houses and hotels situated around an attractive woodland chine leading down to the sea. It has some of the best clifftop views in the area, overlooking the broad waters of Poole Bay.

BOURNEMOUTH

THE HERBERT HOME, WESTBOURNE 1892 / 31371

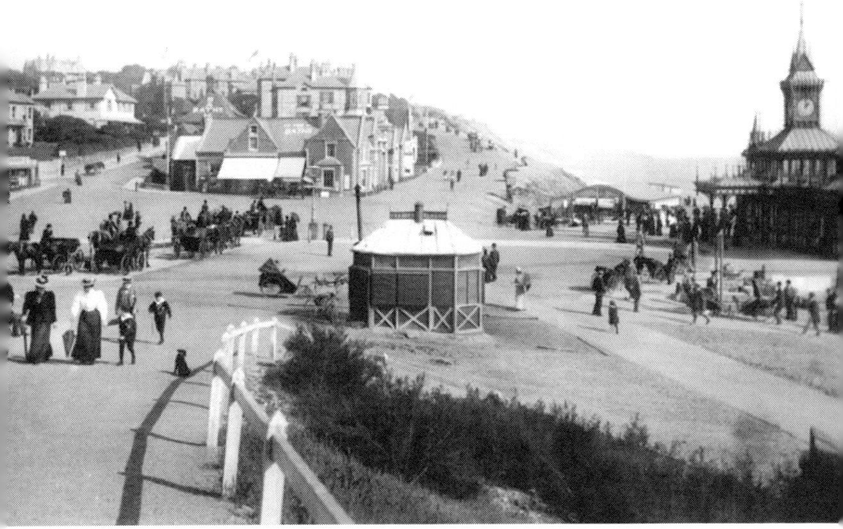

Because of the unstable nature of the cliffs above Bournemouth's beaches, many of the buildings were built at a distance from the cliff edge. Here we are looking at East Cliff towards Boscombe and Southbourne from the rising gradient of West Cliff.

BOURNEMOUTH

EAST CLIFF FROM THE WEST 1897 / 40556

This view, with well-clad visitors strolling along the beach and sailing boats drawn up on the shore, shows a south coast beach before development and formalisation changed its character. Even so long ago, the trappings of a modern seaside resort were starting to appear.

BOURNEMOUTH

EAST CLIFF 1897 / 40562

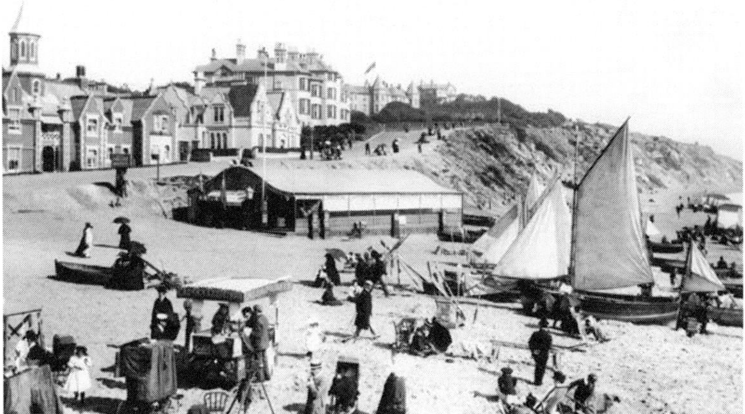

Early visitors preferred to stay in the hotels and villas in this area, within easy walking distance of the sea. The parasols were used to provide shade from the bright sun. The mildness of the climate first attracted visitors to the town, and it rapidly acquired a reputation as a place beneficial to consumptives.

BOURNEMOUTH

WEST CLIFF FROM THE EAST 1897 / 40558

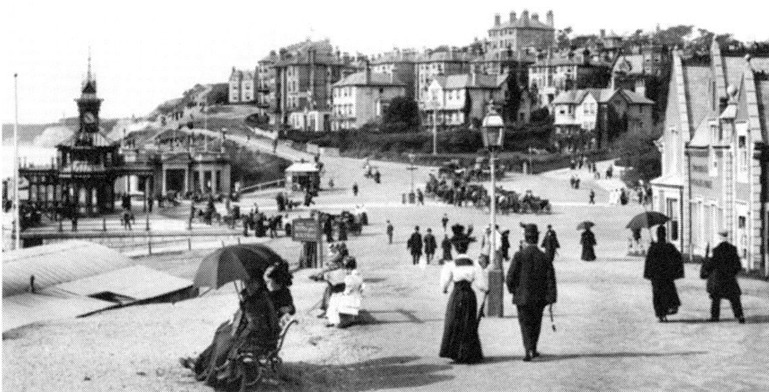

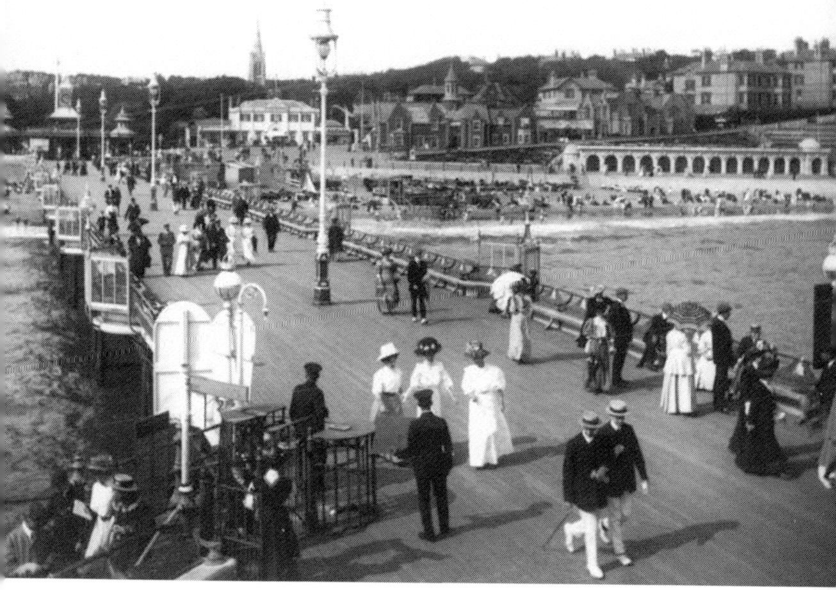

Bournemouth Pier stands above the original mouth of the River Bourne. Its construction marked the town's commitment to its role as a resort. Only a century after its foundation, the town was already dominating the skyline and its beaches were among the most crowded on the south coast. Thomas Hardy described the town as 'Sandbourne' in his novel 'The Hand of Ethelberta', and immortalised it in 'Tess of the D'Urbervilles' as 'the city of detached mansions'.

BOURNEMOUTH

THE PIER 1908 / 61180

Given that this part of the coast had a small number of harbours, the coastal pleasure boats were moored alongside Bournemouth's Pier. Here we see the Swanage boat about to set sail on a calm day.

BOURNEMOUTH

THE SWANAGE BOAT 1908 / 61183

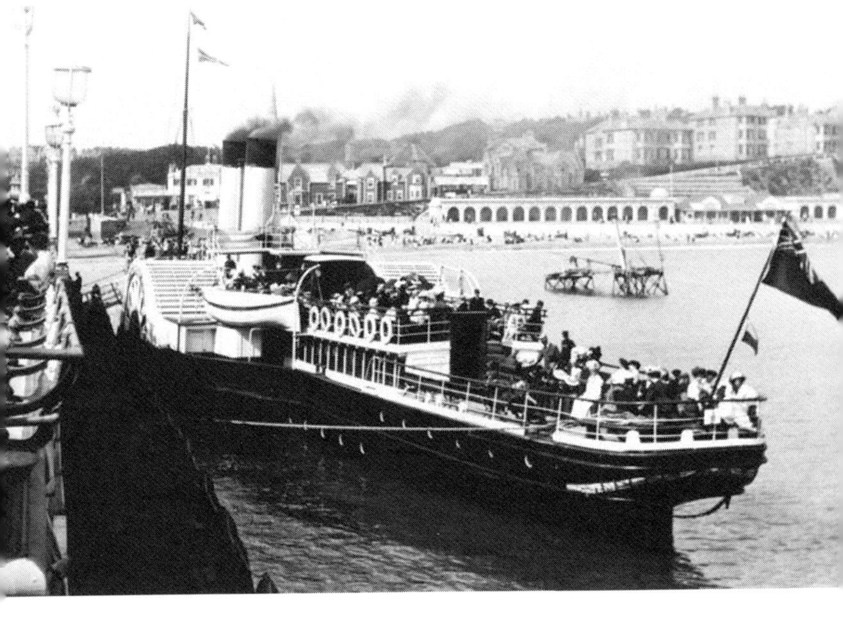

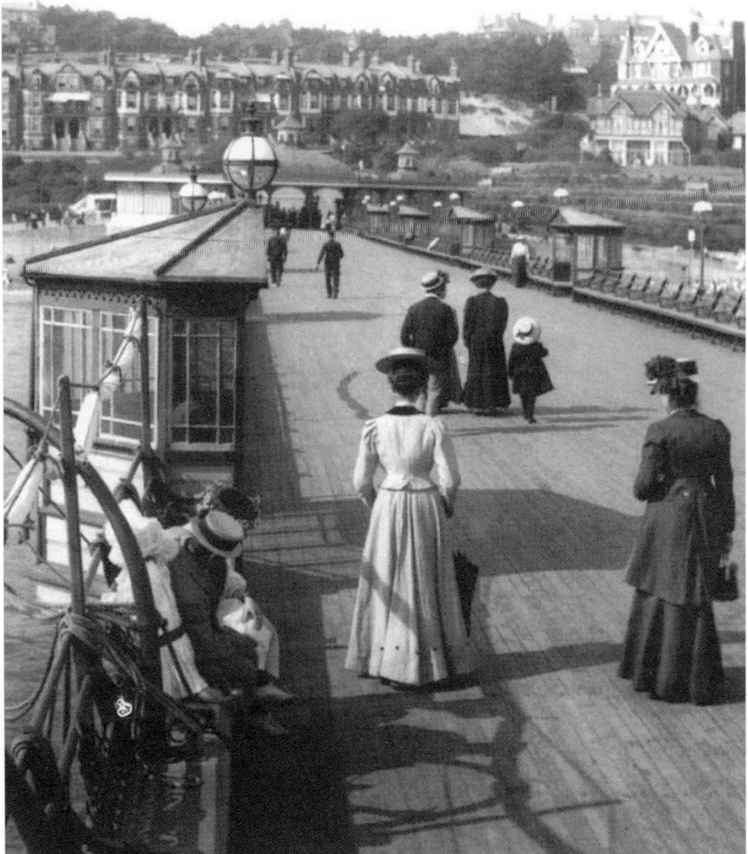

BOSCOMBE

THE PIER 1908 / 61191

Boscombe developed to the east of Bournemouth in mid-Victorian times, attracting the wealthy and fashionable including Sir Percy Florence Shelley, the son of the poet. Mineral springs added to Boscombe's attraction for those seeking an improvement to health, though it never became the spa that it aspired to be.Like Bournemouth's Pier, the struture at Boscombe was severely damaged in the Second World War, but both have been sympathetically restored. A third pier at Southbourne did not survive.

BOSCOMBE

FROM THE PIER 1918 / 68076

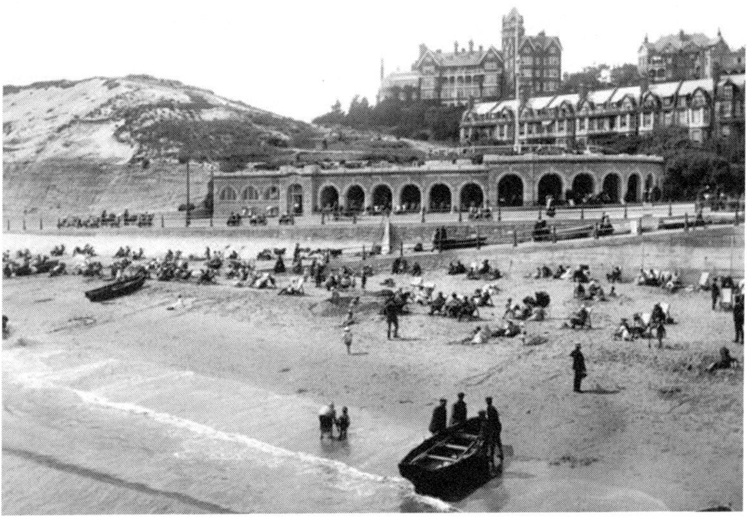

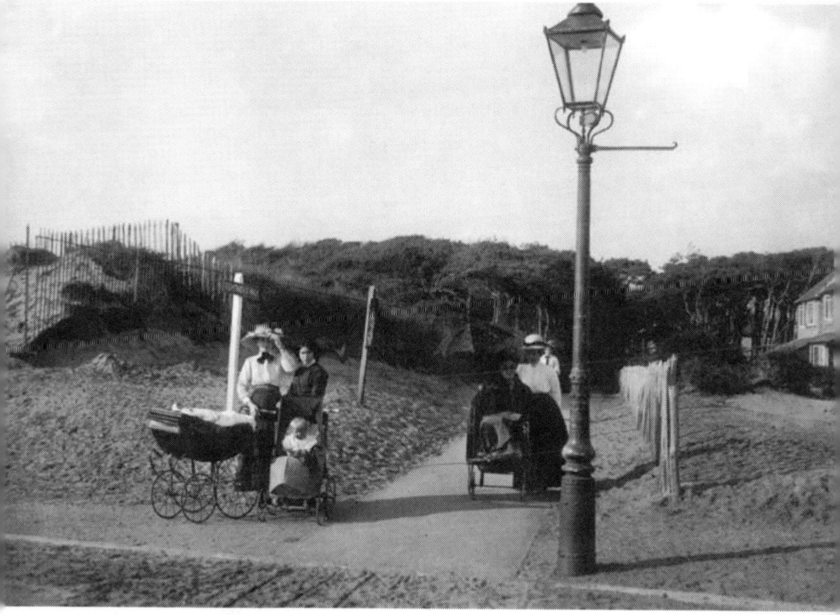

Boscombe was built across a wooded chine (a wide ravine) that led down to the sea; these features are common along this coast. Since this photograph was taken, many of the quieter strolls have been formalised into pretty flower-filled gardens, where tourists and locals alike can sit and contemplate on pleasant days.

BOSCOMBE

FISHERMEN'S WALK 1913 / 66138

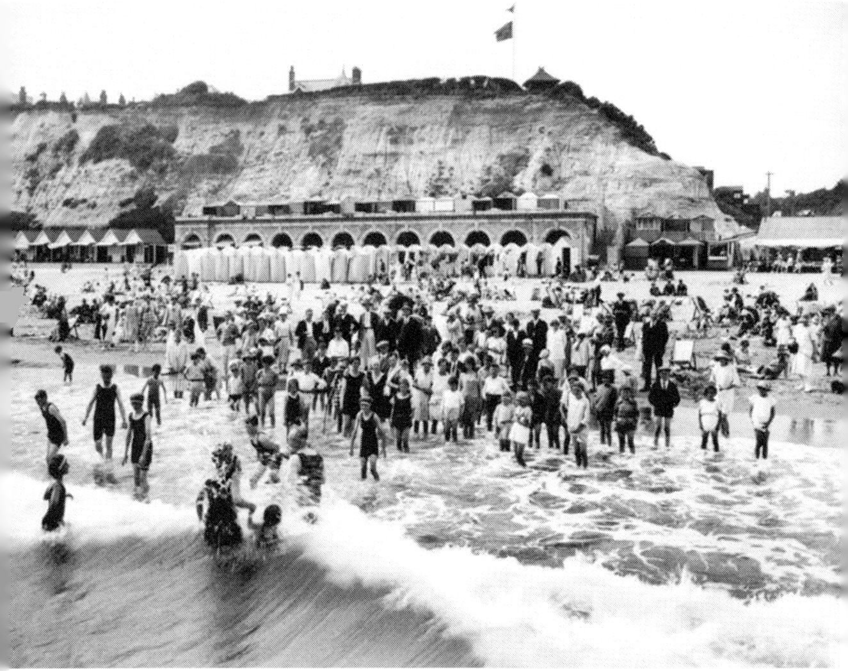

By the 1920s, bathing costumes had become more practical than those shown in the previous illustrations, and the bathing machines had become redundant in favour of smaller kiosks and tents. Beach huts, which could be rented on a weekly basis, have become a feature of the seaside scene.

BOSCOMBE

THE BATHING BEACH 1925 / 78783

Christchurch Road, seen here as it enters Boscombe, must be one of the longest streets in England, as it runs the full distance between Bournemouth and Christchurch. Though quiet in the year of the photograph, it became notorious for traffic jams in the next century.

BOSCOMBE

CHRISTCHURCH ROAD 1892 / 31381

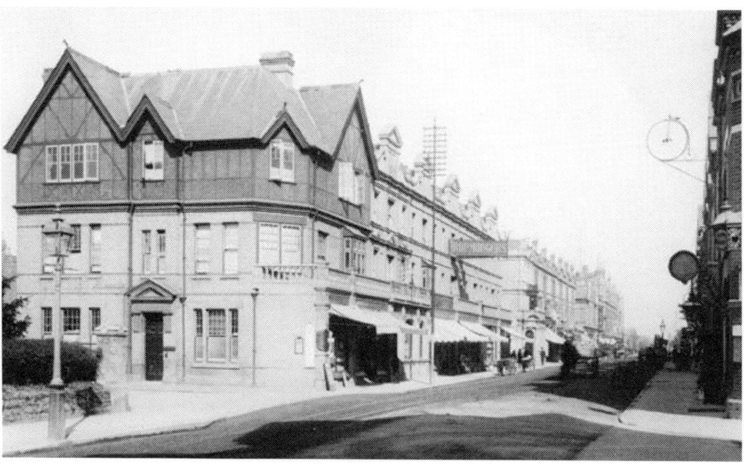

The Arcade became one of the most fashionable shopping streets in the area. The gothic architecture remained an enthusiasm for builders and architects throughout the late Victorian period.

BOSCOMBE

THE ARCADE 1892 / 31380

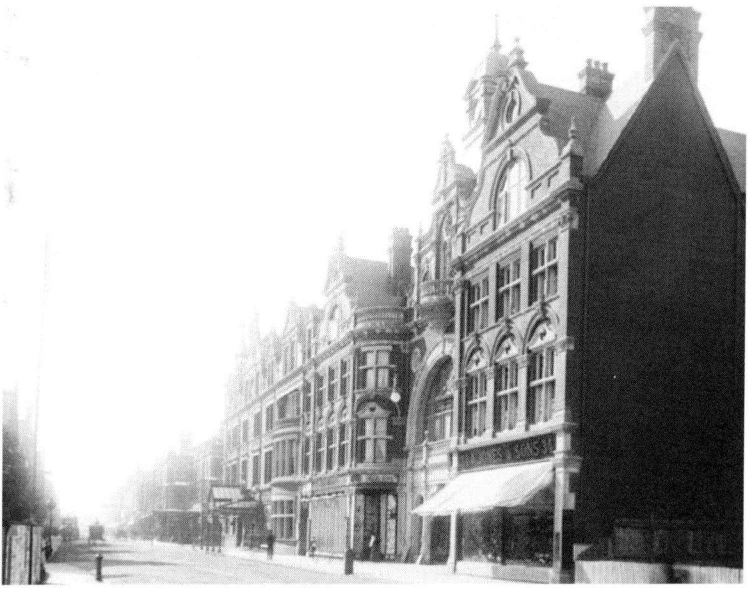

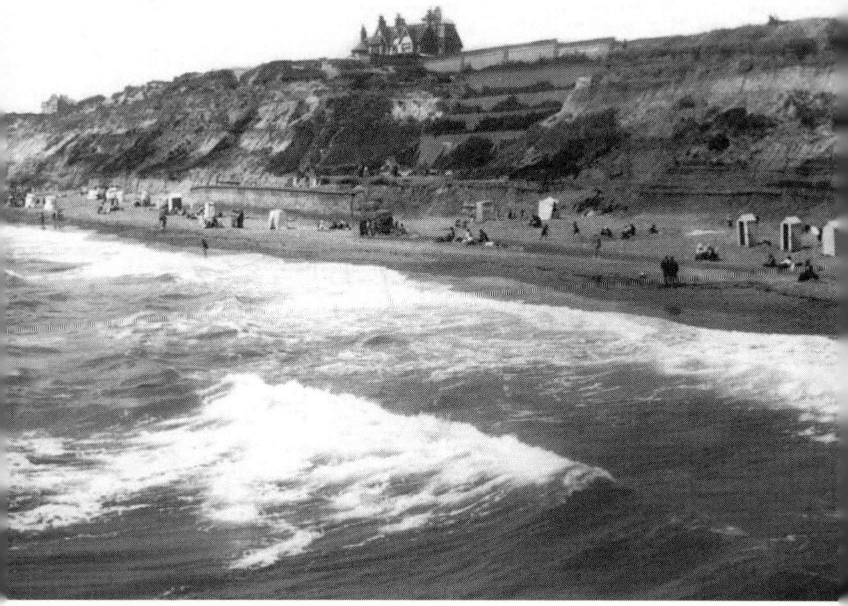

Southbourne has an unfortuate place in aviation history as the scene of the air crash that killed the pioneer pilot Mr Rolls, of Rolls Royce fame, in 1910. Rolls was the first person to die in a British air accident. The downlands above the cliffs were popular with early aviators until Southbourne became too built up.

SOUTHBOURNE

FROM THE PIER 1908 / 61203

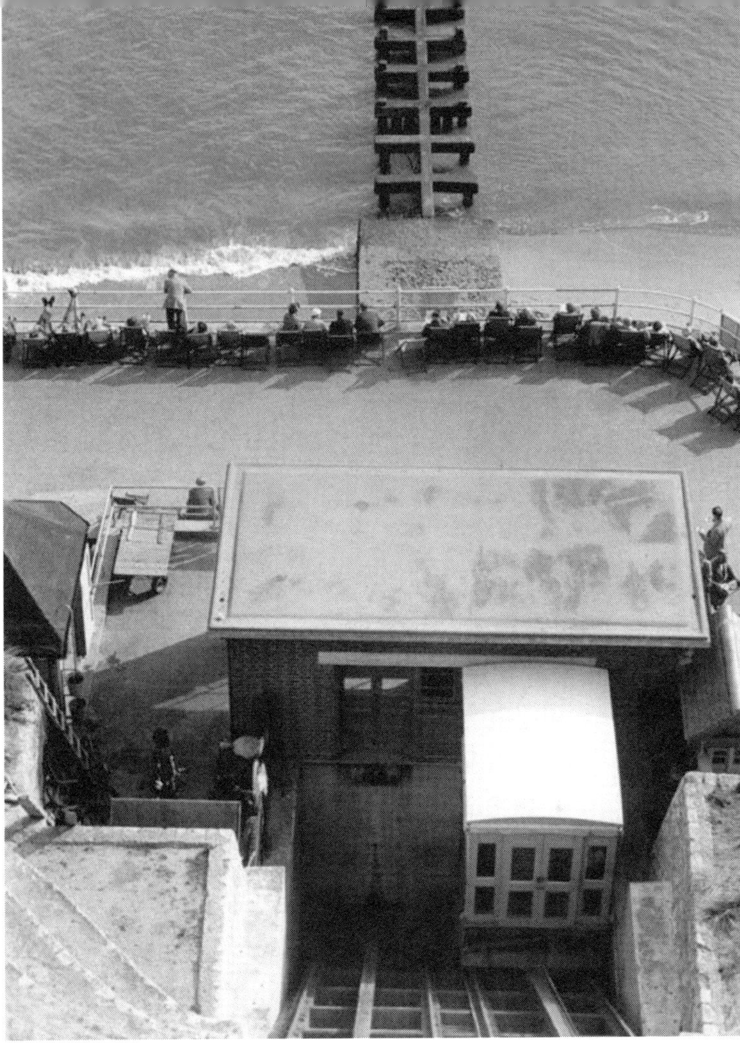

SOUTHBOURNE

THE CLIFF RAILWAY c1955 / S153115

Some local people tried to continue making a living in the old trades. Small fishing boats would be launched off the beaches for many years after the first tourists arrived; fishermen would also offer boat trips to visitors.

SOUTHBOURNE

FISHERMAN'S WALK 1922 / 72714

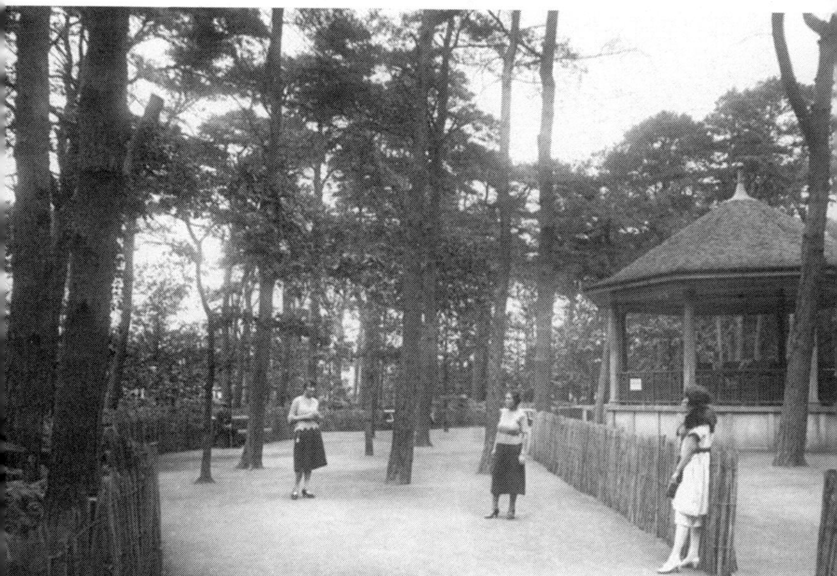

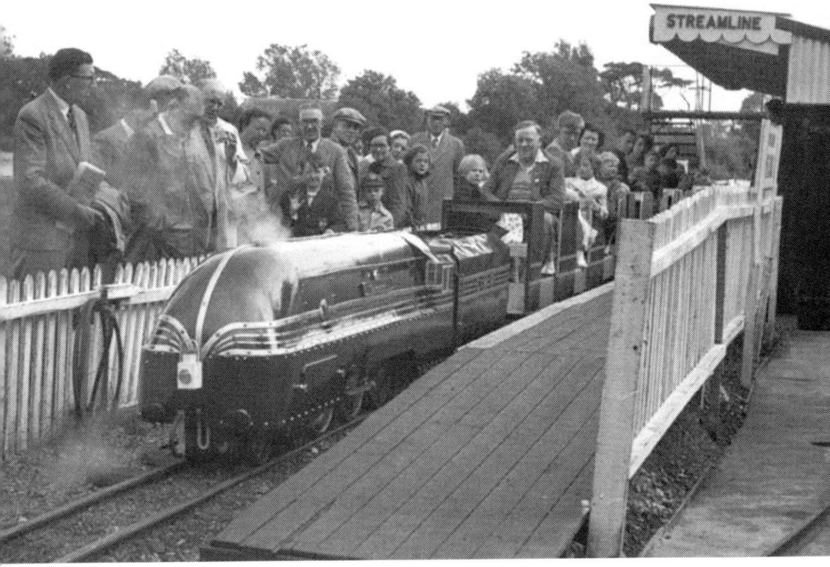

The holiday camp phenomenon had been developed by Billy Butlin before the Second World War. By the 1950s, the popularity of a cheap and cheerful holiday camp atmosphere brought thousands of visitors to camps like Wick Ferry each year. The model steam train was a popular attraction, as it took campers along the edge of the Holiday Park.

CHRISTCHURCH

WICK FERRY HOLIDAY CAMP C1955 / C99166

Highcliffe Castle, near Christchurch, once one of the grandest stately homes in Hampshire, has been undergoing major restoration in recent years to bring it back to its former glory. The grade 1 listed building was built by Lord Stuart de Rothesay in the Romantic style between 1830 and 1835, employing the famous London architect William Donthorpe.

HIGHCLIFFE

THE CASTLE 1900 / 45059

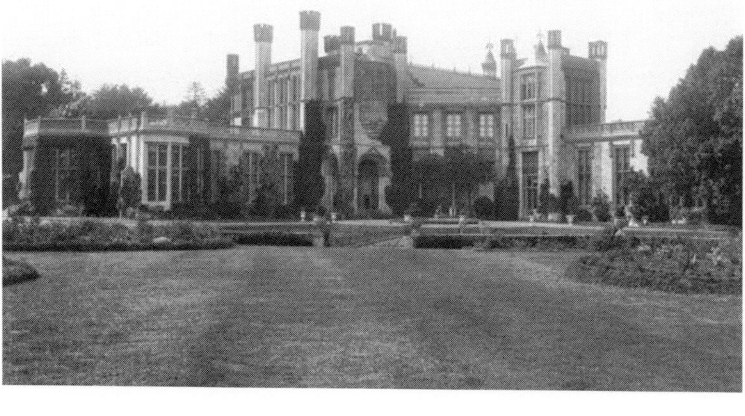

Looking out onto Christchurch Bay, Mudeford remains the centre of the fishing industry in the area. Sheltered from the worst of the Channel gales by Hengistbury Head, Christchurch Harbour empties into the sea between the quays and Mudeford sandbank. Salmon are netted and crabs caught here by local fishermen, and dinghies sailed by locals and holidaymakers alike.

MUDEFORD

THE SAND HILLS 1934 / 86276

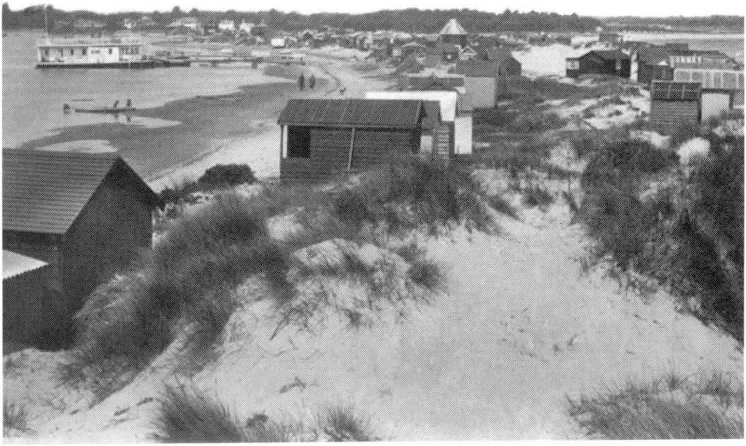

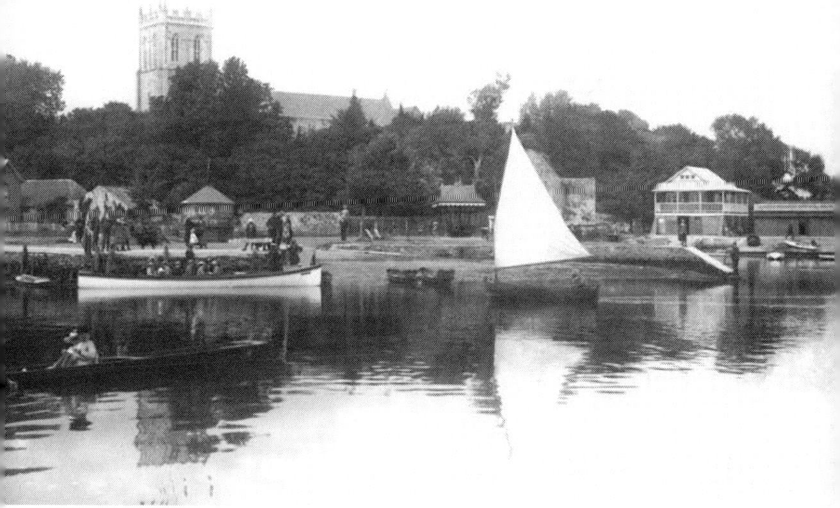

Christchurch (or Christchurch Twyneham, to give the town its old name) is one of the oldest settlements on the south coast, probably being in existence even before the Romans settled in the shelter of Hengistbury Head sometime after AD43. It owes its continued existence to the patronage of the Saxon kings of Wessex and its adoption by the later Normans.

CHRISTCHURCH

THE RIVER 1918 / 68052

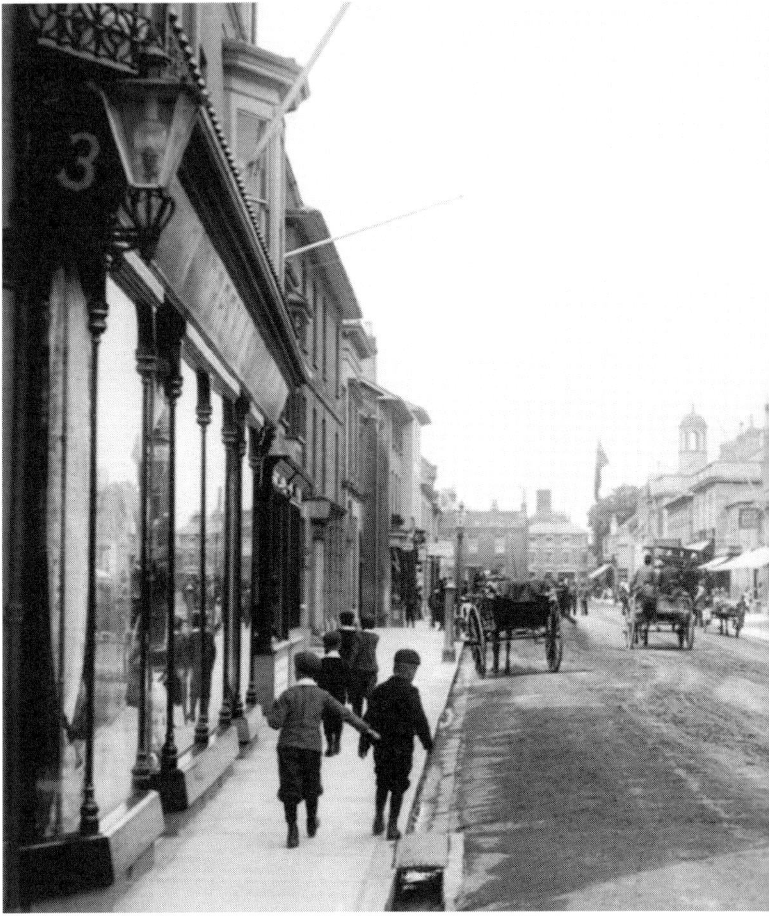

CHRISTCHURCH

HIGH STREET 1900 / 45043

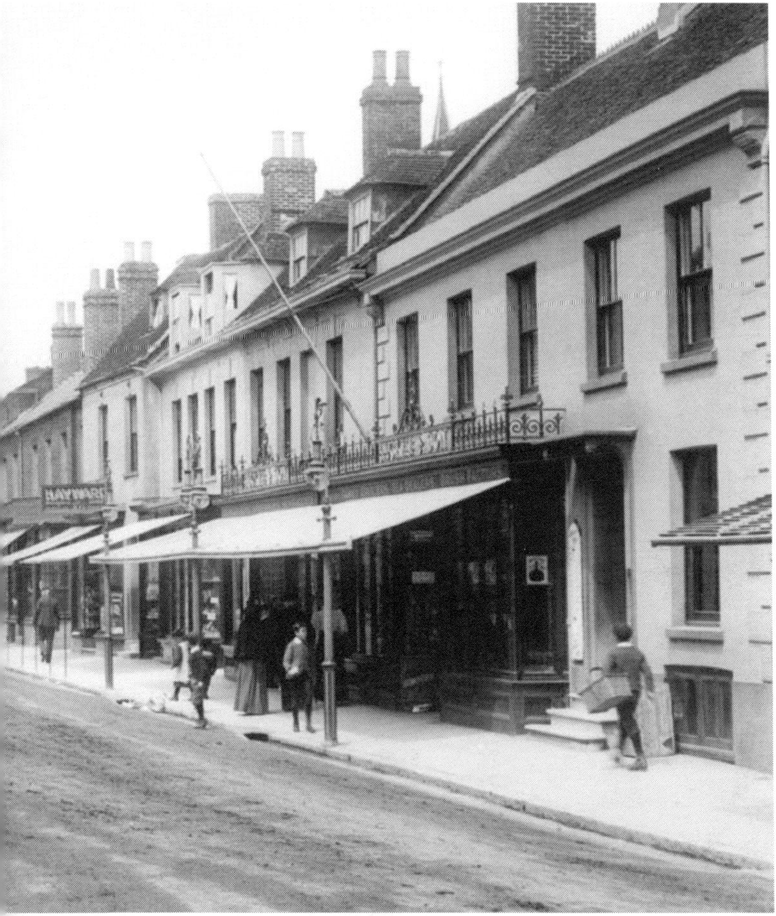

The street has much fine Georgian and Victorian architecture. Leading up to the castle and priory, the High Street has always been the focus of the town. It is interesting to remember that trade prospered in this historic street for centuries before a single house stood in neighbouring Bournemouth.

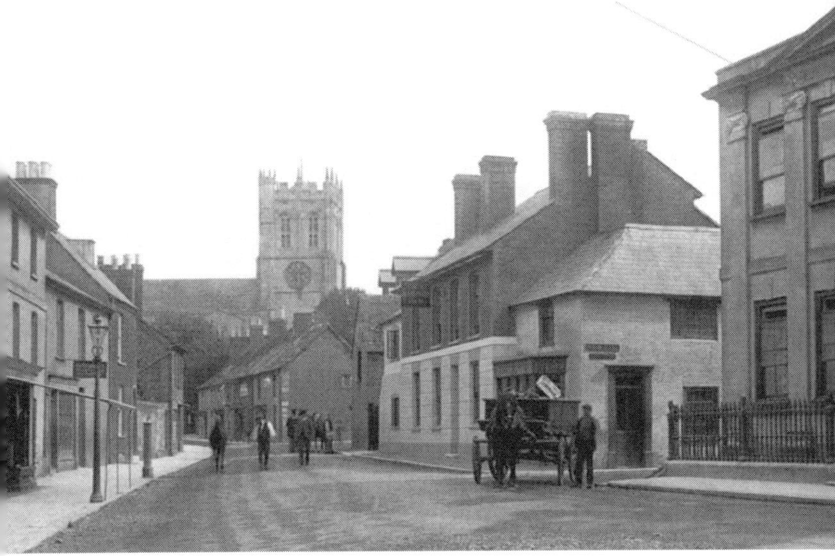

This view shows a working community—the town still thrives today. Until around 1900, fishing was still a major industry in Christchurch, though its port never really developed beyond the present simple harbour. The Saxon church was demolished by the Normans in 1095 and the present building, the longest parish church in England, built in its place.

CHRISTCHURCH

CHURCH STREET 1900 / 45053

Christchurch stands on two rivers, the Stour and the Avon, and gets its old name of Twyneham from the Anglo Saxon, meaning 'the town between the rivers'. Here the ferryman at Blackwater pulls the ferry across the water using a rope as propulsion.

CHRISTCHURCH

BLACKWATER FERRY 1900 / 45048

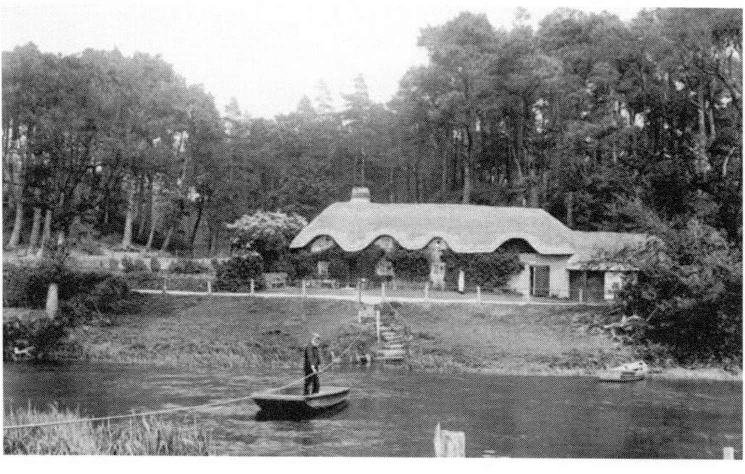

INDEX

PLEASE HELP US BRING FRITH'S PHOTOGRAPHS TO LIFE

Our authors do their best to recount the history of the places they write about. They give insights into how particular towns and villages developed, they describe the architecture of streets and buildings, and they discuss the lives of famous people who lived there. But however knowledgeable our authors are, the story they tell is necessarily incomplete.

Frith's photographs are so much more than plain historical documents. They are living proofs of the flow of human life down the generations. They show real people at real moments in history; and each of those people is the son or daughter of someone, the brother or sister, aunt or uncle, grandfather or grandmother of someone else. All of them lived, worked and played in the streets depicted in Frith's photographs.

We would be grateful if you would tell us about the many places shown in our photographs—the streets with their buildings, shops, businesses and industries. Describe your own memories of life in those streets: what it was like growing up there, who ran the local shop and what shopping was like years ago; if your workplace is shown tell us about your working day and what the building is used for now. With your help more and more Frith photographs can be brought to life, and vital memories preserved for posterity.

We will gradually add your comments and stories to the archive for the benefit of historians of the future. Wherever possible, we will try to include some of your comments in future editions of our books. Moreover, if you spot errors in dates, titles or other facts, please let us know, because our archive records are not always completely accurate—they rely on 150 years of human endeavour and hand-compiled records.

So please write, fax or email us with your stories and memories. Thank you!

CHOOSE ANY PHOTOGRAPH FROM THIS BOOK

for your FREE Mounted Print. Order further prints at half price

Fill in and cut out the voucher on the next page and return it with your remittance for £2.50 for postage, packing and handling to UK addresses (US $5.00 for USA and Canada). For all other overseas addresses include £5.00 post and handling. Choose any photograph included in this book. Make sure you quote its unique reference number eg. 42365 (it is mentioned after the photograph date. 1890 / 42365). Your SEPIA print will be approx 12" x 8" and mounted in a cream mount with a burgundy rule line (overall size 14" x 11").

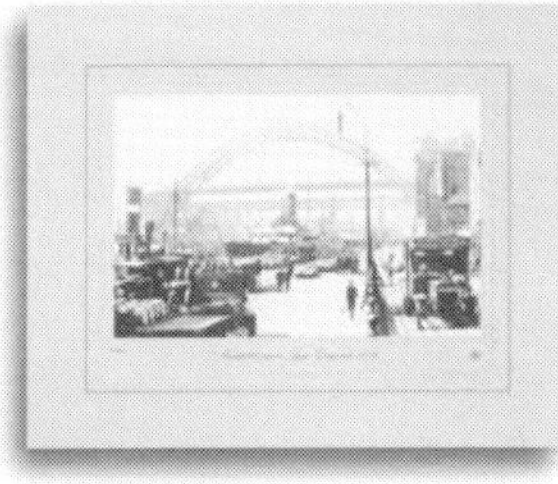

Mounted Print
Overall size 14 x 11 inches

Order additional Mounted Prints at HALF PRICE - If you would like to order more Frith prints from this book, possibly as gifts for friends and family, you can buy them at half price (with no extra postage and handling costs) - only £7.49 each (UK orders), US $14.99 each (USA and Canada).

*** IMPORTANT!**

These special prices are only available if you order at the same time as you order your free mounted print. You must use the ORIGINAL VOUCHER on the facing page (no copies permitted). We can only despatch to one address.

Have your Mounted Prints framed (UK orders only) - For an extra £14.95 per print you can have your mounted print(s) framed in an elegant polished wood and gilt moulding, overall size 16" x 13" (no additional postage).

FRITH PRODUCTS AND SERVICES

All Frith photographs are available for you to buy as framed or mounted prints. From time to time, other illustrated items such as Address Books, Calendars, Table Mats are also available. Already, almost 50,000 Frith archive photographs can be viewed and purchased on the internet through the Frith website.

For more detailed information on Frith companies and products, visit

www.francisfrith.co.uk

For further information, trade, or author enquiries, contact:

The Francis Frith Collection, Frith's Barn, Teffont, Salisbury SP3 5QP

Tel: +44 (0) 1722 716 376 Fax: +44 (0) 1722 716 881 Email: sales@francisfrith.co.uk

Voucher *for FREE and Reduced Price Frith Prints*

Do not photocopy this voucher. Only the original is valid, so please fill it in, cut it out and return it to us with your order.

	Picture ref no	Page number	Qty	Mounted @ £7.49 UK @$14.99 US	Framed + £14.95 (UK only)	US orders Total $	UK orders Total £
1			1	**Free of charge***	£	$	£
2				£7.49 ($14.99)	£	$	£
3				£7.49 ($14.99)	£	$	£
4				£7.49 ($14.99)	£	$	£
5				£7.49 ($14.99)	£	$	£
6				£7.49 ($14.99)	£	$	£
	Please allow 28 days for delivery				*** Post & handling**	$5.00	£2.50
					Total Order Cost US $		**£**

Title of this book ....

I enclose a cheque / postal order (UK) for £ .... $ ....
payable to 'Francis Frith Collection' (USA orders 'Frith USA Inc')

OR debit my Mastercard / Visa / Switch (UK) / Amex card / Discover (USA) *(credit cards only on non UK and US orders)*, card details below

Card Number

Issue No (Switch only) Valid from (Amex/Switch)

Expires Signature

Name Mr/Mrs/Ms ....

Address ....

....

....

Postcode/Zip...................................... Country ....

Daytime Tel No ....

Valid to 31/12/06

PAYMENT CURRENCY: We only accept payment in £ Sterling or US $. If you are ordering **from any other country, please pay by credit card**, and you will be charged in one of these currencies.

Send completed Voucher form to:

UK and rest of world - The Francis Frith Collection, Frith's Barn, Teffont, Salisbury, Wiltshire SP3 5QP England

USA and Canada orders - Frith USA Inc, 11447 Canterbury Lane, Parker, Colorado, 80138 USA

If you need more space, please write your address on a separate sheet of paper.